CRITICAL THINKING AND THE ACADEMIC STUDY OF RELIGION

SCHOLARS PRESS
Studies in the Humanities

CRITICAL THINKING AND THE ACADEMIC STUDY OF RELIGION

by

Richard Penaskovic

Scholars Press
Atlanta, Georgia

CRITICAL THINKING AND THE ACADEMIC STUDY OF RELIGION

by

Richard Penaskovic

©1997
Scholars Press

Library of Congress Cataloging in Publication Data
Penaskovic, Richard.
    Critical thinking and the academic study of religion / by Richard
Penaskovic.
        p.   cm. — (Scholars Press studies in the humanities)
    Includes bibliographical references.
    ISBN 0-7885-0360-X (paper : alk. paper)
    1. Religion—Study and teaching. 2. Critical thinking.
I. Title. II. Series: Scholars Press studies in the humanities
series.
BL41. P464   1997
200'.71—dc21   97-9824
                                           CIP

Printed in the United States of America
on acid-free paper

Contents

Acknowledgments

This book represents the results of five years of research and twenty three years of teaching undergraduates. In publishing it I have been prompted by the conviction that a new way of teaching religious studies is required in this age of information overload.

Those of us in religious studies have in the past focused almost exclusively on content instead of endeavoring to teach our students how to think. The explicit teaching of critical thinking depends less on *what* is taught, than on *how* it is taught. This book shows how critical thinking may be accomplished within the context of religious studies.

To anyone writing a book, it helps immensely to have an angel around the house. That is why I dedicate this book to my wife, Nancy. It is also dedicated to my aunt, Helen Lipinski and to the memory of Dora Bolger, both of whom took me in when I had nowhere to go.

I am indebted to the criticism and encouragement provided by William Busquist, Professor of Psychology at Auburn University, Brennan Hill, Professor of Theology at Xavier University, Cincinnati and Denise Lardner Carmody of the University of Santa Clara. I am grateful to my editor at Scholars Press, Dennis Ford, and to Micky Logue, Professor Emeritus of Journalism at Auburn University. I owe, however, a special debt of gratitude to Jay Lamar, Coordinator of the Center for the Arts and Humanities at Auburn University, without whose editorial help and encouragement this book would not have been completed.

I wish to acknowledge the help of various individuals who assisted me throughout various drafts of this manuscript: Elsie Reynolds, Michelle Fannin Moore, Brandy Juhl, Jane Dunkelberger, Steve Murray, Lisa Lester and Bobbie Gordie. I am grateful to Dr. Paul Parks, Provost of Auburn University for setting aside funds for the improvement of teaching and to the Teaching-Learning Committee, chaired by Margaret Miller, for a Teaching Grant supported by the University Concessions Board of Auburn University. This grant enabled me to attend a workshop on Process Education at Corning Community College in Corning,

New York, conducted by Dan Apple of Pacific Crest Software, Corvallis, Oregon, which refined my thinking on cooperative learning. I learned a great deal about cooperative learning from the members of my small group: Gina Albertalli, Pete Bacalles, Debra Borden, Jayne Peaslee, and Jan Scott.

Preface

This book contains a few brushstrokes on an immensely large canvas. Educational reform will not come about through sweeping changes of institutionally mandated programs but through the small improvements that faculty make in their own courses. Faculty alone have the power to make revolutionary changes in teaching/learning.

This book offers some suggestions for changing college teaching, particularly as it applies to the academic study of religion. However, it should not be looked upon as a panacea. The ideas found in this book may not fit neatly into your course, but they can serve as basic templates that can be modified according to your concrete needs. The more variations instructors are familiar with, the more alternatives they will have in their repertoire to solve the continually changing problems they encounter in teaching.

I have based this book on theories of learning found in the writings of cognitive psychologists. For those who wish to explore the theory behind this book more carefully, I recommend the book *Instructional Design: Implications from Cognitive Science* by Charles K. West, *et al* Englewood Cliffs, New Jersey: Prentice Hall, 1991.

The principles that support cognitive theories of learning may be understood by contrasting them with the behaviorally-oriented philosophy of learning that forms the basis of many current teaching methods. For the behaviorist, knowledge can be sorted into several components and taught through practice and reward. Learning proceeds by memorizing facts, rules, and principles. Higher-order thinking skills such as decision-making, critical thinking, and synthesis are not considered basic to learning. Students have a passive role to play in the acquisition of knowledge; faculty an active one.

Cognitive theories of learning, on the other hand, put the student at the center of knowledge acquisition. Learning is the process by which students become more expert in a particular domain. It is the process by which students interpret and assimilate new information, relate it to what they already know, and organize it for later retrieval. In other words, students are active learners, responsible for regulating the learning process by applying a host of learning strategies. Learning proceeds in recursive phases rather than in a linear manner.

The basic assumption in this book is this: by looking at their teaching from another perspective, that of critical thinking, faculty will be helped to discover aspects of it which were previously hidden. One must desist from viewing teaching as course coverage. Instead, one must see it as helping students learn. This book invites you to reframe the roles of both instructor and student. The focus of one's courses in religious studies must shift from the content to the student. If this is done, the classroom then becomes the locus where students assume an active role in learning, in contradistinction to being passive observers of the ongoing scene as in the behaviorist approach to learning.

I believe that the process of thinking must become the content of the curriculum in religious studies. Content ought to be selected because it contributes to the thinking process. In the course of writing this book I have become convinced that the development of the intellect, the production of knowledge, problem-solving, decision-making, and meta-cognition must become the subject matter of instruction.

To turn students into critical thinkers is not an easy task. This book will provide pointers on how to make a start in what is a complicated process. By turning students into critical thinkers and active learners, instructors are released from the responsibility of providing all classroom instruction. They will find out that students can learn a great deal on their own and from their peers in a well-designed course.

The ideas found in this book have been tried and tested in my own classes over the past five years. Both my students and I have learned from our successes and from our failures. We have come to see that failure should not be viewed in terms of an unmitigated disaster but as an opportunity to learn. The challenge comes in trying to turn negatives into positives.

Scholars in the humanities, in general, and in religious studies, in particular, approach their work with an excitement of exploration, a questioning attitude, and a dedication to staying on the cutting edge of their particular discipline. This book suggests that if scholars bring these same attitudes to their teaching, they will approach it with new zest. At least this has been my experience in writing this book. I now approach teaching in a qualitatively different way than I did.

In sum, the goal of this book is to empower professors of religious studies to be adventuresome in their teaching. Many ideas are offered in hopes that faculty will adapt their professional knowledge to what their students need. My stated goal is to free teachers to be both inspired and inspirational.

Please contact me at 310 Thach Hall, Auburn University, AL 36849-5205 or E-mail me at penasri@mail.auburn.edu if you have suggestions for improving this text or if I can be helpful to you in any way as you attempt to infuse critical thinking into your courses in Religious Studies.

1

What Is Critical Thinking?

"Most people would sooner die than think. In fact, they do."
                                                        Bertrand Russell

Introduction

A recent national report on education concluded that colleges fail to teach students to think.[1] Why are undergraduates not learning to think? At the heart of the problem is the effectiveness of college and university teaching. We presently have a distorted reward system that makes research more important than teaching. The language of the academy is instructive: professors speak of research *opportunities* and teaching *loads*, never the reverse.[2] Research has these payoffs: respect of one's peers beyond one's campus, enhanced reputation on campus, and access to funds. But however poorly rewarded teaching is, it is our business, and many reports suggest that critical thinking should be a basic part of undergraduate education. They agree that the primary experiences undergraduates should gain are to reason well, to recognize when reason and evidence are insufficient, to discover the legitimacy of intuition, and to subject data to probing intellectual analysis.[3]

This chapter deals with three main questions: 1) What is thinking? 2) What is critical thinking? 3) What are the mental operations or intellectual skills that constitute critical thinking? We will address these questions by drawing concrete examples from the academic study of religion.

---

[1] "Integrity in the College Curriculum," *The Chronicle of Higher Education*, 13 February 1985, 12–30. See Gail A. Caissy, "Curriculum for the Information Age" *Educational Horizons* 68 (Fall 1989): 44. Diane F. Halpern writes that recent tests have shown that only 25% of college freshmen have the skills needed for logical thought See *Thought and Knowledge: An Introduction to Critical Thinking*. Third Edition (Mahwah, New Jersey: Lawrence Erlbaum Associates, Publishers, 1996) 32.

[2] Ibid., 15.

[3] Ibid., 18. California Executive Order #338 provides that at least nine semester units must be devoted to improving oral and written communication skills and critical thinking abilities. See Kerry S. Walters, "Critical Thinking in Liberal Education: A Case of Overkill?" *Liberal Education* 72 (Fall 1986): 244.

What Is Thinking?

Thinking refers to our active, organized effort to make sense of the world and to clarify our understanding.[4] It is the process by which knowledge (understood as organized human experience) is acquired, developed, tested, and applied. The logical approach to thinking defines it as "right reasoning." The psychological approach, on the other hand, defines thinking as the selection, organization, and transformation of information as a person makes sense of various situations.[5]

Both knowledge and thinking are used in everyday life. There are two main approaches to thinking: the formal, logical approach as opposed to informal or everyday reasoning. Formal reasoning follows a set of rules within a self-contained problem. Informal reasoning, on the other hand, challenges us to address the problem in ways that are consistent with one's attitudes, values, and *Weltanschauung*. In everyday or informal reasoning problems are ill defined, have no clearly correct answer, and lack established procedures for solving the problem. A homemaker buying food in the supermarket uses the same processes and the same kinds of knowledge as the economist analyzing market trends.[6]

Metaphors and Analogies

Thinking is difficult to define precisely, and definitions for thinking may be less useful than metaphors and analogues depicting thinking. For instance, one may think of the mind as an attic, a place to collect items and to store them until needed. Like an attic, the mind is an intriguing place to explore: one can poke through old nooks and crannies to see what one can rediscover and use again. But undisciplined minds may gather intellectual cobwebs as unused attics do dust.

The mind may also be thought of as a computer, taking in information bit by bit, storing it in short-term memory, and then organizing and filing it into long-term memory. Information can be retrieved by accessing it through a central processor in the brain, and the thinking person can

---

4 John Chaffee, *Thinking Critically* (Boston: Houghton Mifflin Company, 1985), 49. Some researchers identify three kinds of thinking: analytical, creative, and practical. However, traditional schooling rewards only analytical thinking. See Robert J. Sternberg and Louise Spear-Swerling, *Teaching for Thinking* (Washington, D.C.: American Psychological Association, 1996), 5–33, and Mark Weinstein, "Critical Thinking: Expanding the Paradigm," *Inquiry: Critical Thinking Across the Disciplines* Vol. XV, No. 1 (Autumn, 1995), 23–39. For a listing of some of the recent studies on critical thinking (along with brief abstracts) arranged by categories, see Jeris F. Cassel and Robert J. Congleton, *Critical Thinking: An Annotated Bibliography* (Metuchen, New Jersey: The Scarecrow Press, 1993).

5 Ernest Mc Daniel and Chris Lawrence, *Levels of Cognitive Complexity: An Approach to the Measurement of Thinking* (New York: Springer-Verlag, 1990), 1.

6 Eugene J. Meehan, *The Thinking Game: A Guide to Effective Study* (Chatham, New Jersey: Chatham House Publishers, Inc., 1988), 1.

use the information to solve problems. But such a metaphor of the mind has a downside. It drives a wedge between thinking and feeling, creating an "apartheid of the mind," an artificial separation of thoughts and feelings.[7]

One can also think of the mind as a kaleidoscope. When new ideas and other information enter the brain, they are encountered by an already well-formed, constantly changing scheme or kaleidoscopic structure. The brain makes sense of new information in terms of its existing mental maps or schemes. We may imagine that these mental maps are stored as an elaborate group of lights that flash first one way and then another, while patterns are created by altering the circuitry. In this metaphor the human mind is a dynamic, ever-changing light board.[8]

Jot down the metaphors that you use to describe the mind. Go over your list with a colleague who shares your interest in teaching religious studies. Which analogue offers the greatest potential as a metaphor for thinking about thinking?

What Is Critical Thinking?
There is no agreement among scholars on a definition of critical thinking, although a group of scholars led by Peter Facione has proposed a consensus statement, which will be discussed later in this chapter. Some scholars find the lack of a clear, universally accepted definition of thinking disturbing, but living with conceptual ambiguity should not be difficult for scholars working in religious studies. After all, there is no universally accepted definition of religion.

A Discipline and a Competency
Critical thinking is both a discipline and a competency. As a discipline it is drawn from philosophy and psychology. Pertinent to the educational reform movement of the 1970s, the concept came to be applied to classroom instruction, where it resulted in improved teaching/learning.

Critical thinking is best seen as a competency, central to mastering subject matter and to developing other intellectual abilities.[9] The rest of this section examines various definitions of critical thinking, including the one we find most helpful in the academic study of religion.

---

[7] Dan Kirby and Carol Kuykendall, *Mind Matters: Teaching for Thinking* (Portsmouth, New Hampshire: Boynton/Cook Publishers, 1991), 13.

[8] Ibid., 14.

[9] George Hanford, "Critical Thinking: a Field, a Discipline, a Subject, Or a Competency?" *Inquiry: Critical Thinking Across the Disciplines* 10 (May 1993): 13. See Maurice Finocchiaro, "Critical Thinking, Critical Reasoning, and Methodological Reflection," *Inquiry: Critical Thinking Across the Disciplines* Vol. XV, No. 4 (Summer, 1996), 66–79.

Definitions of Critical Thinking

Most definitions of critical thinking have been proposed by and bear the disciplinary marks of either philosophers or psychologists. Philosopher Peter Facione defines critical thinking as the ability to properly construct and evaluate arguments.[10] Critical thinkers, he says, have the ability to detect hidden assumptions and presuppositions. They are also able to distinguish arguments from emotional appeals.

Facione's definition may appeal to philosophers, particularly to logicians. However, a critical-thinking course that stresses "the ability to properly construct and evaluate arguments" may teach students to analyze arguments yet fail to address their tendency to maintain existing beliefs or their inability to weigh evidence objectively. In other words, Facione's definition is too narrow; critical thinking encompasses a great deal more than the analysis and evaluation of arguments.

One may ask whether the analysis of arguments is central to reasoning in all academic disciplines. English, according to one study, relies heavily on the analysis and evaluation of arguments.[11] However, education and psychology value the generation of alternatives. In religious studies analysis and evaluation of arguments are important in biblical studies and in theological ethics, but in the psychology of religion the generation of alternatives is critical. Religious studies uses a multiplicity of methods, and it is difficult to say that one method is effective to the exclusion of others.

Another problem with limiting our definition of critical thinking to an analysis of arguments is that such a definition does not accommodate tacit, or implicit, knowledge. Whereas explicit knowledge is set out in words, maps, or mathematical formulae, tacit knowledge is unformulated and thus does not lend itself to the orderly construction and evaluation characteristic of the former. Those who grapple with a particular discipline for many years have a tacit understanding of words and symbols that is unavailable to the neophyte. For example, a seasoned teacher who is having difficulty with a particular class will know through past experience how to deal with the situation. However, the beginning teacher may be overwhelmed by the problem. The critical role of tacit knowledge in problem-solving should not be neglected.

---

[10] Peter Facione, "Testing College-Level Critical Thinking," *Liberal Education* 72 (Fall 1986): 222.

[11] Joanne G. Kurfiss, *Critical Thinking: Theory, Research, Practice and Possibilites.* ASHE-ERIC Higher Education Report No. 2 (Washington, D.C.: George Washington University, 1988), 3.

Well-Structured vs. Ill-Structured Problems

For some researchers critical thinking comprises the mental processes, strategies, and representations people use to solve problems, make decisions, and learn new concepts.[12] For them, critical thinking embraces two kinds of problems: well-structured problems and ill-structured problems. Such subjects as accounting, mathematics, and the hard sciences deal with well-structured problems in which there usually exists one, correct answer.[13]

Ill-structured problems, on the other hand, have no single solution, e.g., What career should I choose? Should I get married or remain single? Everyday problems deal with informal reasoning as opposed to the formal, logical approach to reasoning, which follows a set of rules within a bounded or self-contained problem.

Some knowledge domains such as history, the social sciences, psychology, and religious studies are not very logical and may be called ill-structured. The relative structure does not run throughout all the knowledge in a discipline. For instance, some parts of ill-structured domains can be well structured and some parts of well-structured domains can be ill structured.

Reasonable Evaluation

Critical thinking may also be defined as thinking marked by reasonable evaluation. A critical thinker gives a reasoned evaluation of a book, a movie, or a work of art, along with explanation. Proponents of this definition argue that critical thinking involves such skills as careful judgment, sustained reflection, decision-making, problem-solving, and the production of ideas, plans, arguments, experiences, and alternatives.[14] There is a lot to be said for this definition of critical thinking. Critical thinking certainly involves a reasonable evaluation. If one says that critical thinking involves such skills as careful judgment, sustained reflection, decision-making, problem-solving, and the production of ideas, plans, arguments, experiences, and alternatives, I wonder how these

---

12 See John Follman, "Critical Thinking Definitions," *Inquiry: Critical Thinking Across the Disciplines* 8 (October 1991): 4. Cf. Shirley W. Schiever, *A Comprehensive Approach to Teaching Thinking* (Boston: Allyn and Bacon, 1991).

13 Lower-order thinking occurs when learners are asked to receive or recite factual information or to use rules and algorithms through repetitive routines. See Fred M. Newman and Gary G. Wehlage, "Five Standards of Authentic Instruction," *Educational Leadership* 50 (April 1993): 9.

14 Kenneth Hawes, "Understanding Critical Thinking," in *Varieties of Thinking: Essays from Harvard's Philosophy of Education Research Center*, ed. V.A. Howard (New York: Routledge, 1990), 48.

skills relate to each other. Is critical thinking an umbrella term which includes all of these skills? Or is critical thinking a skill much like problem-solving, decision-making, and careful judgement? There seems to be no consensus among educators about the exact relationship found between these higher order thinking skills. For my own part, I see critical thinking as an umbrella term covering such skills as decision-making, problem-solving, and careful judgement.

A Consensus Statement on Critical Thinking.
An interactive panel of experts led by Facione has come up with a consensus statement regarding critical thinking and the ideal critical thinker. The groups used a qualitative research methodology called the "Delphi Method" in which panelists work toward consensus by sharing reasoned opinions and reconsidering the opinions with regard to arguments offered by other experts. A total of forty six scholars, all of them leading researchers in the area of critical thinking, came up with this consensus statement or definition of critical thinking.

"We understand critical thinking to be purposeful, self-regulatory judgment which results in interpretation, analysis, evaluation, and inference, as well as explanation of the evidential, conceptual, methodological, criteriological, or contextual considerations upon which that judgment is based."[15]

There are several difficulties with this statement or definition of critical thinking:

1. A definition should be simple. This definition is very complex. In fact, it needs to be explained at length in order to be fully understood.
2. This consensus statement has not been accepted by other scholars working in the field of critical thinking. In fact, I have not seen any mention of it in the books that have been written about critical thinking since it appeared in 1990.

Chaffee's Definition of Critical Thinking.
To think critically, says John Chaffee, is to be careful or meticulous in examining our own thinking and that of others in order to improve our understanding.[16] I have taken Chaffee's definition to heart in this book. Critical thinking means to think actively and for ourselves. To think critically means to take an active attitude toward the situations encountered

[15] Peter A. Facione, "Critical Thinking: A Statement Of Expert Consensus For Purposes of Educational Assessment And Instruction," *Eric Document* 315423 (1990), Table I, 3.
[16] John Chaffee, 51.

in life, rather than waiting for things to happen or simply allowing others to tell us what to do.

Critical thinking involves the careful exploration of an issue or a situation. It is the very opposite of doing whatever pops into our minds. For example, I recently was fishing with my daughter, age sixteen. I stood up in the boat to retrieve a lure which was caught on a tree, and before I knew it I was treading water. The boat had overturned in a flash. My daughter and I were able to get right back into the boat which started to sink as it filled with water.

Neither of us panicked, even though we knew there was an alligator in our small lake. I had my daughter leave the boat and get help because (a) the boat was sinking under the weight of two persons combined with the large amount of water it had taken on, (b) we were close to shore, and (c) darkness was fast approaching. I told her to bring back a bucket so I could bail out the boat. However, I was able to get most of the water out of the boat, then retrieve the oar and some of our fishing paraphernalia, and make it back to shore with one paddle.

How was this an instance of critical thinking? I did not wait for help but made some fast decisions myself (thinking actively and for myself). I got into the boat even though it was filled with water because it was safer there than in the water with the alligator. I knew the alligator was not near shore so that it was safe for my daughter to walk through the water to shore and summon help. I did not swim immediately for shore but stayed with the boat, even though it was so full of water that it was very unstable. In other words I carefully explored the situation and made some fast decisions which proved to be correct.

This definition of critical thinking is admittedly very general and, consequently, needs to be made operational and applied to the academic study of religion, but it has the virtue of practicability. And it will allow us to approach the important task of delineating what critical thinking means in terms of specific intellectual skills or mental operations. This chapter concerns itself more with the operational definition of critical thinking than it does with an abstract and theoretical definition. In the following section I attempt to give the definition of critical thinking some specificity.

Critical Thinking & Religious Studies
Critical thinking is both a frame of mind and a number of specific mental operations or intellectual skills, each of which combines analysis and evaluation. The core of these operations is as follows:

1) Detecting bias and identifying unstated assumptions. The word *bias* may be understood in two ways. *Bias* may mean predisposition, tendency, or leaning. It often has a pejorative connotation, suggesting close-mindedness, prejudice, or irrational rigidity. In this section *bias* is used in this second sense.[17]

Detecting Bias

To encourage students to be alert to bias, one may ask questions about the required texts for a course. I ask students if the authors of the textbooks have a bias in favor of a particular religion. Can they give concrete examples of bias from the text, citing chapter and verse? For instance, are two chapters of the text devoted to one religion while another major religion is ignored? Do the authors of the text put down marginal or alternative religions by labeling them cults or sects? Is such labeling acceptable in the academic study of religion?

Do the authors clearly state their aims in the preface? What do they fail to say? Do they assume any prior knowledge about religion on the part of students? Is the text written for undergraduates or for scholars in the field? How can we tell? Similar questions may be asked of television evangelists or any religious journal. For instance, do certain publications systematically create enemies, setting up categories of "us" against "them," insiders versus outsiders, our group versus the enemy?

2) Explicitly raising the questions "What do we know. . . ?" "How do we know. . . ?" "What is the evidence for. . . ?" when studying a body of material or approaching a problem. Many students need to be pushed and pulled into raising questions as "Why do we believe. . . ?" "How do we know. . . ?" Multiple-choice questions often force students into memorizing definitions; yet the habit of inquiry can be cultivated. One must take time to encourage students to ask hard questions. An effective way to do this is to teach them by example.

Raising Difficult Questions

Instead of asking questions that depend on simple recall, pose such questions as "What is the evidence for the claim that a literal reading of the Bible is inadequate?" "How do we know how the Israelites lived?" "Why do Christians believe that Christ was both God and man simultaneously?" "How do we know that the Koran is the inspired word of God?" "Are there any criteria for deciding that one religion is better than another?" "Are they all equally valid?"

You may also ask what evidence we have for positing the existence/ nonexistence of God. How do scholars in religious studies arrive at their

---

[17] Richard Paul, *Critical Thinking: What Every Person Needs to Survive In a Rapidly Changing World* (Rohnert Park, CA: Sonoma State University, 1990), 170.

conclusions? How does their methodology vary? How do specialists in religion learn to use the methods of special disciplines such as history, psychology, and philosophy to address such complex issues as the question of human origins or the question of religious pluralism?

3. Thinking actively and for ourselves. Because of the knowledge explosion, which we will discuss in the "Barriers to Critical Thinking" chapter, it is impossible to teach students all that they need to know. For this reason education must help individuals to their own intellectual feet, teaching them how to learn and instilling in them a desire to make learning a lifelong endeavor.

What It Means to Think Critically

Critical thinking means adopting an active attitude toward the obstacles one encounters in life rather than passively waiting for things to happen. One who thinks critically does not simply accept what others say but asks for reasons and evidence to support those views. To think critically means to analyze and evaluate the views and prejudices we were brought up with, to retain some and reject others.[18]

Examining the Evidence

We should reflect on how we arrived at our views and examine the reasons and evidence that support them. For example, I was taught by my church that practicing birth control was wrong. I accepted this for the first twenty years of my life until I went to study at Innsbruck, Austria, and came into contact with other students who convinced me that there were instances where the practice of birth control could be justified. These students had convincing arguments. I came to the conclusion that I could no longer accept the view of my church based on an unquestioning acceptance of authority.

Thinking for Ourselves

To think actively and for ourselves requires the capacity to judge when understanding has been reached and to make inferences and draw conclusions from acquired knowledge. This includes testing one's thinking for internal coherence and consistency. By encouraging students to think for themselves, we help them discover their own minds. They can then dispense with us and come to their own conclusions.

Self-Discipline

It requires self-discipline to think for oneself. To be self-disciplined one must gather, assess, synthesize, and apply information for oneself. We

18 John Chaffee, 59.

can teach and nurture these skills by giving students first-hand experience with scholarship in religious studies. Annotated bibliographies, book reviews, and term papers take students into the stacks and into the ongoing dialogues of the discipline. As they respond to the course requirements, they learn to gather material, organize it, and evaluate the arguments they find in it. As they encounter scholars' critiques of other scholars, they learn to be critical in their own reviews.

On Making Connections

Students are further motivated to think for themselves when they are taught how religious studies connects with other disciplines. Many students who register for a course in religion are not majors in religion. Hence they need to learn to integrate their knowledge of religion with their own majors and/or other academic subjects. The instructor can facilitate this process in two ways: 1) by asking students during the first week of class what their majors are and by making reference to these subjects in lectures/ assignments and 2) by suggesting that students do their term papers or book reviews on topics that are interdisciplinary in nature or that deal with the boundaries between such disciplines as spirituality and psychotherapy, religion and literature, or science and religion.

4. Determining the reliability of a source/statement.   One must use reliable sources of information in formulating conclusions. Those who think critically are suspicious of sources that have a vested interest in influencing belief, are not in a position to know, or are contradictory. Critical thinkers compare alternative sources of information, note areas of agreement and disagreement, and search out further information when the sources disagree. They are aware that preconception influences observation; that is, we often see what we expect to see and fail to see things we are not looking for.

Consulting Experts

In addition to examining conflicting partisan views in studying religion, it may be necessary to learn what neutral experts say on a topic. If a student is writing a report on the Christian Scientists, it would be important to compare Christian Science literature with the writings of non-partisan researchers on the movement. In determining the reliability of a source, various questions need to be raised. Has the source been dependable in the past? Is the source in a position to know? Joseph Smith, for example, the founder of the Church of Jesus Christ of the Latter Day Saints, insisted that the angel, Moroni, appeared to him in 1827 and revealed the location of golden plates upon which the Book of Mormon was written. Is there any external evidence supporting the claims of Joseph Smith?

Analyzing Statements
Asking probing questions may be useful in analyzing a statement. In the Hindu religion Lord Krishna professes to be an incarnation of the god Vishnu. On what basis does Lord Krishna make this claim? Does Lord Krishna have anything to gain by claiming to be an avatar of Vishnu? What kinds of knowledge would Lord Krishna have to provide to convince someone that he is, in fact, an incarnation of Vishnu?

5. Evaluating arguments and evidence. In everyday life an argument means a dispute or a quarrel. In this section, the word *argument* means one or more statements that are used to support a conclusion. These statements are called reasons or premises. For this reason arguments may be called the "giving of reasons."[19]

Questioning Authorities
In order to help students evaluate arguments and evidence, we must encourage them to question the views of a teacher, a famous scholar, a textbook, or another knowledgeable student. Many students realize how little they know about the subject of religion and are quick to defer to all kinds of supposed experts. Hence students may assume that the source of an opinion guarantees its substance. They also assume that the professor already knows all the answers. How many times have your students said, "I don't know if this is the answer you're looking for, but. . . ."?

Provide Opportunities
As a general rule, the best way to help students evaluate arguments and evidence is to provide opportunities for them to do so. Point out inconsistencies in arguments and gaps in available information by drawing examples from the course texts, or use a class period to evaluate the comments made by a guest speaker.

Some students may be turned off by a guest speaker, sometimes for superficial reasons. They may be perplexed, for instance, by a Hare Krishna because his head is shaved and he wears Indian clothing. Because he is from a different religious tradition, they may be only too

---

[19] See Diane Halpern, *Thought and Knowledge: An Introduction to Critical Thinking*, 3rd ed. (Mahwah, New Jersey: Lawrence Erlbaum Associates, Publishers, 1996), 168. See Douglas Walton, "New Methods for Evaluating Arguments," *Inquiry: Critical Thinking Across the Disciplines*, Vol. XV, No. 4 (Summer, 1996), 44–65.

willing to criticize him. Students must get beyond speakers' exteriors and hone in on the arguments they use to ground their point of view.

Examining Arguments
In order to gauge the effectiveness of an argument, three aspects or criteria of an argument must be examined. The first criterion concerns the consistency and acceptability of the premises.[20] Premises are the statements or reasons that support a conclusion, and they are consistent when they do not contradict one another. Premises are acceptable when we can reasonably believe that they are true. For example, I know that Hawaii is an island even though I have never walked around Hawaii myself to make sure that it is surrounded by water on all sides. What we believe to be true depends on common or shared knowledge and on experts' statements.

The second criterion deals with the relationship between the premises and the conclusion. It answers the question, Does the conclusion follow from the reasons offered? It may be difficult at times to determine the relatedness between the premises and the conclusion. Former President Ronald Reagan believes that abortion is wrong. Reagan is a highly intelligent person. Conclusion: Abortion should be condemned as morally wrong. Although President Reagan served as president and may be an intelligent person, these facts do not give him any special expertise in regard to moral questions such as abortion. The conclusion does not follow from the reasons given, hence this argument is invalid.

The Conclusion as a Table-Top
One may think of the conclusion as a heavy marble table-top. It will certainly topple over if supported only by a few toothpicks. Its support requires one or more strong legs, which are the premises or reasons that support the table-top, or conclusion. When the premises provide convincing support for the conclusion, we may say that there are adequate grounds for believing that the conclusion is true.[21]

The Invisible Part
The third criterion in evaluating an argument concerns the unseen part of the argument. It corresponds to the question, What is missing that would change the conclusion? An excellent way to find out what is missing in an argument is to suspend one's viewpoint and argue from the other side. One could then ask what additional information is needed or what premises are missing that would support an opposite conclusion.

20 Ibid., 187.
21 Ibid., 189.

Yugoslavia is currently in the midst of a civil war. One could argue that the United States should become involved in that war because innocent blood is being shed every day in that country. Do we have a moral obligation to intervene for humanitarian reasons, or do we have a moral obligation to keep out of that struggle both because it is a civil war and our national interests are not involved? I also ask students who are pro-choice to argue the case for pro-life and vice versa.

6. *Carefully exploring before making decisions.* A large part of decision-making involves exploring a situation, beginning with the idea that a problem exists. Many decisions have to be made with missing information and hence involve calculated guesses and predictions about future events. Teaching itself may be regarded as a decision-making process. To succeed, teachers must make good instructional decisions.

The Intangibles

Designing a course such as Introduction to Religion often involves many intangibles. The instructor does not always know the size of the class, the maturity level of the students, or the students' previous knowledge of the discipline.

How does one go about making a decision when all the data are not in? One should begin by clearly defining the problem and laying out a set of alternative solutions from which to choose. By phrasing the problem in several different ways, one can improve the way in which the decision is made. In other words, by changing the focus of the problem, other alternatives may emerge.

Designing a Course

For example, in designing a course one can focus on effective teaching: How can I best teach the Introduction to Religion course? Sub-questions emerge: How much do I know about the various topics to be covered in the course? How much preparation time will I have in which to learn quickly those parts of the course unfamiliar to me? What are the library resources available to me and to my students for the proposed course? What resources in the community, including audio-visuals and guest speakers, can I call upon for help? What other courses do I have to teach that semester, and how will that work impinge upon my proposed course? What family matters will restrict the time I have available for course preparation?

Gathering Information

In order to make a sound decision one must gather information before selecting alternatives. A decision, of course, is only as good as the information upon which it is based. The registrar may be able to tell you how many students have signed up for a course and what their majors are. A veteran professor can offer insight into what students are like at a particular institution. Almost any decision can be improved upon by some diligent research.

Reducing Risk

What about making decisions that may involve potentially disastrous outcomes?[22] There are ways to avoid, manage, or reduce risks. Take the case of junior faculty members who want to teach in new ways but fear that senior faculty members in the department will deny them tenure or promotion if they do so. The junior faculty members may meet with the department chairperson, describe their dilemma, and solicit an opinion. The chairperson may be able to assure the faculty members that this is an imagined rather than a real worry. If the class is team-taught, junior faculty members might invite a senior faculty member to join them. Sometimes it only takes a bit of imagination to avoid, manage, or reduce risks. The same tactics may be applied to other problems in academic life.

7. Discussing our ideas (and those of others) in an organized way.   A primary goal of higher education in the United States during the eighteenth and nineteenth centuries was to enable students to present their ideas convincingly and powerfully to others. Yet many students today have difficulty writing well and speaking persuasively. As teachers we need to encourage students to write well, so that they can present solutions to present-day problems convincingly. Students should be encouraged to translate information in their fields to a variety of audiences. In order to do this, students need a thorough knowledge of their subject matter and the ability to simplify.

Writing and Its Complexity

Writing itself, as every English teacher knows, is an exceedingly complex activity. Writing has intricate rules (grammar) that cannot be violated without paying the cost in understanding. Writing not only helps us organize our thoughts, but it also helps us move beyond stereotypical ways of thinking. As St. Augustine wrote in the *De Trinitate*: "I must also acknowledge, incidentally, that by writing I myself have learned much that I did not know."[23]

---

22 Ibid., 325.

23 *The Works of Saint Augustine: The Trinity*, trans. Edmund Hill, ed. John E. Rotelle (Brooklyn, New York: New City Press, 1991), 127.

Some Basic Rules of Writing
Although writing is a complex activity, one can make a start by teaching students to follow some basic rules: 1) state the main idea; 2) explain the main idea; 3) provide illustrations of the idea and offer examples, arguments, and evidence to support it; and 4) draw a conclusion.

8. Being open to new ideas.   Most of us are prone to believe that our perception of reality *is* reality. Critical thinkers, who realize that no one has a monopoly on the truth, are able and willing to look at new ideas and viewpoints. In order to understand a problem or situation, we need to consider the viewpoint of others. This is harder to do in practice than to state theoretically. A few examples may clarify the difficulties involved in transcending our own point of view.[24]

Changing Our Minds
Being open to new ideas and points of view means being willing to risk the possibility of changing our minds about something important to us. What would induce us to change our opinion on a particular issue? New information may be presented to us that calls into question our previous knowledge. Thirty years ago we were ignorant about the multiple health hazards connected with inhaling secondary smoke from those around us. Today we know better how serious smoke in any form is to our general health.

New insights that we gain through experience may encourage a change of opinion. When I began teaching twenty years ago, I thought that students would be genuinely interested in learning for learning's sake. I now realize that most students are primarily grade conscious.

As we gain experience, we may realize that we have been raised with certain prejudices. We may, for instance, see women as inferior to men or vice versa, or we may have grown up with certain biases against specific ethnic, racial, or religious groups. As we mature, we may see the conflict between what we have been taught and the experiences we have had with a particular minority group. We have to be flexible enough to modify our views, if we are, in fact, critical thinkers.

9. Making Sound Judgments.   In Chapter Three we will discuss the three levels of learning: declarative knowledge, the skills level, and metacognition. Judgment has to do with the second, or skills, level, which deals with procedural knowledge or strategic knowledge. Procedural knowledge means knowing how to use declarative knowledge to execute a skilled performance like writing a critical book review. Procedural

[24] John Chaffee, 66.

knowledge makes it possible to do something in one's subject area. It includes knowledge of how information is obtained, analyzed, and communicated in a discipline.[25]

Different Codes

Different disciplines have different "codes" of procedural knowledge. Some aspects of the code are formalized: the scientific method, for instance. Other codes are implicit. Procedural knowledge is rarely taught because it remains tacit knowledge for experts in a particular discipline. But procedural knowledge is paramount when we try to answer the question: How do students acquire the skills and dispositions that are required in order to think in the mode of the discipline?[26]

Such a question is particularly difficult to answer in religious studies because no one methodology dominates the field. Rather, there exists a multitude of methodologies, such as the psychological perspective, the sociological method, the historical view, the phenomenological perspective, and the hermeneutical method, to name just a few.

Sound Judgment

How does one form sound judgment? The best way to begin is to take a wide and liberal compass, to read and think a great deal on a wide variety of subjects. Anthropology, history, art, literature, ethics, and rhetoric exercise the faculty of judgment. The elements of general reason are not found in any one kind of study. One who would know the idiom of sound judgment must read it in many books.[27] Careful observation is another way to form sound judgment. This involves the attempt to go beyond surface appearances and to get at the heart of a problem.

Sound judgment corresponds with our best idea of what it means to have a cultivated mind. It gives one strength in any subject, enabling one to seize the strong point in a particular discipline. Judgment teaches one to see reality as it really is, to go straight to the point, to disentangle a skein of thought, detecting what is sophistical and discarding what is irrelevant.

10. Metacognition or Thinking about Thinking.   *Metacognition* is the technical term in cognitive psychology for thinking about thinking. The litera-

[25] Joanne G. Kurfiss, 40.

[26] Ibid., 4.

[27] John Henry Newman, *The Idea of a University*, ed. I. T. Ker (Oxford: Clarendon Press, 1976), 153.

ture on education speaks of it as "critical reflection" or as a "literacy of thoughtfulness."[28]

Metacognition

Metacognition means developing self-consciousness about one's own thinking processes. In order to attain this self-consciousness, one must stand back and recognize the strategies or processes one is using. One must then invoke those processes most helpful to the problem at hand and provide the basis for the conscious transfer of reasoning methods from familiar to unfamiliar contexts.[29]

An Example of Metacognition

An example may illustrate thinking about thinking. In writing this chapter I had to decide how much of the literature in cognitive psychology had to be read before writing about the definition of critical thinking. It was also necessary to assess and monitor the approach I took in writing this chapter. I had to answer the question, How could I most effectively tell my colleagues in religious studies about metacognition and critical thinking without resorting to jargon?

Control Strategies

Metacognition involves not one but several control strategies such as making plans, setting goals, asking questions, taking notes, observing the effectiveness of one's efforts, and taking corrective action.[30] For example, the first draft of this chapter did not exhibit a strong organizational structure or argument. It was more a series of reflections which lacked coherence. The revised draft contains an argument and has a much stronger organizational structure than the first draft.

The present draft was difficult to write for several reasons. First, scholars do not agree on any one definition of critical thinking. Second, critical thinking often functions in the literature as a generic term for all

---

[28] Rexford Brown, *Schools of Thought: How the Politics of Literacy Shape Thinking in the Classroom* (San Francisco: Jossey-Bass Publishers, 1991), 232ff. For an excellent discussion of metacognitive strategies for student learning, see Brenda H. Manning and Beverly D. Payne, *Self-Talk for teachers and Students: Metacognitive Strategies for Personal and Classroom Use* (Boston: Allyn and Bacon, 1995), 153–185, and Ruth M. Loring, "Metacognitive Implementation of Journaling: A Strategy to Promote Reflective Thinking," in *Critical Thinking: Implications for Teaching and Teachers: Proceedings of the 1991 Conference*, Wendy Oxman, *et al*, eds. (Upper Montclair, N.J.: Institute for Critical Thinking, 1992), 256–265.

[29] Arnold B. Arons, "Critical Thinking" and the Baccalaureat Curriculum," *Liberal Education* 71 No. 2, (1985): 147.

[30] Joanne G. Kurfiss, 27.

forms of higher-order thinking. Third, writing this chapter involved dealing with an ill-structured problem. There was not one way of organizing and writing this chapter, but several ways. Thus I had to choose the most effective way for my purposes.

Metacognition & Religion

How does the literature on metacognition apply to the academic study of religion? Research indicates that direct strategy training is only partially helpful in increasing performance. Why so? It appears that students lack judgment about which strategies should be applied in diverse situations. For this reason routine problem-solving methods often prove ineffective when dealing with ill-structured problems, be they in engineering, mathematics, or religious studies.

Students must monitor their own learning, using various problem-solving strategies. Only through trial and error will they discover which strategies work best. They must come to see themselves as the object of their own thinking or reflective analysis.[31]

Now that we have in hand a working definition of critical thinking, the question arises about the various barriers that exist to critical thinking. We turn to this question in the next chapter.

Summary

This chapter consists of three closely connected sections. In Part I various definitions of thinking were considered. Thinking was defined as an active, organized effort to make sense of the world and to clarify our understanding. It was suggested that definitions for thinking may be less useful than certain metaphors and analogies. One can, for example, think of the mind as an attic, as a computer, or as a kaleidoscope.

Part II proposed several definitions of critical thinking. Some scholars suggest that critical thinking is both a discipline and a competency. To think critically means to be meticulous in examining our own thinking and that of others in order to improve our understanding. This definition of critical thinking was thought to be very general and was made operational in Part III and illustrated with ten specific mental operations or intellectual skills.

31 Norbert Elliot et al., "Designing A Critical Thinking Model For a Comprehensive Technological University," *Inquiry: Critical Thinking Across the Disciplines* 7 (May 1991): 9. See Patricia M. King and Karen Strohm Kitchener, *Developing Reflective Judgment: Understanding and Promoting Intellectual Growth and Critical Thinking in Adolescents and Adults* (San Francisco: Jossey-Bass Publishers, 1994). The authors have developed the Reflective Judgement Model which overlaps with what other researchers call critical thinking and intelligence.

The core of these operations involves: 1) detecting bias and identifying unstated assumptions; 2) explicitly raising the question: "What do we know and how?" when studying some body of material in approaching a problem; 3) thinking actively and for ourselves; 4) determining the reliability of a source or a statement; 5) evaluating arguments and evidence; 6) carefully exploring a situation or an issue; 7) discussing our ideas and those of others in an organized way; 8) being open to new ideas; 9) making sound judgments; and 10) thinking about thinking, or metacognition. We showed how these ten mental operations apply to the academic study of religion.

2

BARRIERS TO CRITICAL THINKING

"Let what will be said or done, preserve your sangfroid
immovably, and to every obstacle, oppose patience, perseverance,
and soothing language."

Thomas Jefferson

Introduction

If it is important to teach students to think critically, why then do most faculty fail to teach this skill? Why is there such an emphasis on lower-order thinking skills and memorization rather than teaching higher-order thinking skills? And why do most faculty in religious studies lecture when other modes of teaching exist? In sum, why are there so many roadblocks which hinder the introduction of critical thinking into the academic study of religion?

Many barriers militate against the introduction of critical thinking into the academic study of religion. This chapter explores the ten most important of those obstacles and offers suggestions for dissolving them in order to refresh our teaching.

Barrier # 1: Course Coverage

Faculty in religious studies (and most other disciplines) often feel pressure to cover a subject in its entirety, including the minutiae. Such courses as the Old Testament, the History of Christianity, and World Religions contain so much material that faculty feel compelled to lecture. The problem becomes complicated on the graduate level. Students need to be exposed to a vast amount of information in order to do well on M.A. and Ph.D comprehensive examinations.

The Knowledge Explosion
More books have been published since 1945 than in all of the preceding centuries, says Derek Bok in his book *Higher Learning*.[1] Knowledge in the

---

[1] Derek Bok, *Higher Learning* (Cambridge, Mass.: Harvard University Press, 1986), 163. Barry K. Beyer makes a similar point in his book, *Practical Strategies for the Teaching of Thinking* (Boston: Allyn & Bacon, Inc. 1987), 1–9; and Neil Postman, *The End of Education* (New York: Alfred A. Knopf, 1995), 43.

fields of religious studies and theology has become time-sensitive. Textbooks are outdated every five years, and the number of journals in all fields has grown exponentially.

The library at my university has more than 1.7 million physical volumes, 1.9 million items in microformat, and 1.1 million government publications. Incoming freshman do not know where to begin when they are given a research assignment in my Introduction to Religion class. Who can blame them? Even my most conscientious students are faced with the problems of what to read, whom to believe, and how to make sense out of the plethora of publications found in the library.

Specialization makes more and more fields inaccessible to both the lay mind and even to other scholars working in the same field. For example, I know very little about the methodology of the social sciences and would be hard-pressed to teach the Sociology of Religion, even though I have been teaching in the area of religious studies for about twenty years.

Less Is More

Since the curriculum in religion has become too broad for any one person to master and is taught in too shallow a fashion for anyone to know anything in depth, I have come to believe in the adage "less is more." It makes sense to have students learn fewer things in greater depth with greater connectedness than it is to overload them with information. In such a situation, teaching critical thinking skills becomes vital.

It also takes a lot of additional time for faculty to make the switch from a teacher-centered classroom to a student-centered one. In the teacher-centered classroom, faculty lecture, lead discussions, and take an active role in the operation of the class. Students, on the other hand, are put into a passive, dependency position. In cooperative learning students take the initiative, and most of the time is spent in small learning groups.

Cooperative Learning

In cooperative learning, faculty have to spend time teaching students social skills, for example, how to get along in a group, how to communicate effectively, how to listen, and how to solve conflicts constructively. Thus faculty need to take time out from their academic endeavors to teach students these social skills which are vital to learning in small, cooperative groups. Faculty, then, must teach less material in a student-centered classroom because less time is available for covering the material than in a traditional, teacher-centered classroom.

On the other hand, in cooperative learning students reason together to solve a problem or complete an assignment and thus become more involved in communicating and thinking. I would say that the basic reason cooperative learning is becoming popular as a learning technique is that faculty know that it works.

Research on Cooperative Learning
Research suggests that cooperative learning increases academic performance. Why so? Studies demonstrate that interaction with peers, particularly those from diverse linguistic and cultural backgrounds, causes students to make significant academic gains compared with students in traditional settings. Cooperative learning also increases respect for diversity. Students come to appreciate and respect each other when they cooperate to reach a common goal.[2]

Cooperative learning, when used appropriately, motivates students. Students who collaborate on a project experience the joy of sharing ideas and information. Cooperative learning prepares students for the real world, where, in corporations, for instance, people work together to produce a product. Working to get along and combining energies with others are valuable skills in the world of work and of leisure.

There are other positive aspects of cooperative learning. It promotes active learning; that is, students learn more when they are personally engaged in problem-solving and decision-making. Cooperative learning also encourages literacy and language skills. How so? Working in small groups gives students the opportunity to improve speaking skills. This is important especially for students who speak English as a second language.

Cooperative learning also helps faculty make important discoveries about their students' learning. The power of the instructor is multiplied as students assume responsibility for some of the teaching.[3]

Set Goals
As they design a course, faculty need to ask themselves this question: What are the five most important items I want my students to take from

2 Mary Hamm and Dennis Hamm, *The Collaborative Dimensions of Learning* (Norwood, N.J.: Ablex Publishing Corporation, 1992), 2. See Edie L. Holcomb, *Asking the Right Questions: Tools and Techniques for Teamwork* (Thousand Oaks, California: Corwin Press, Inc., 1996), John R. Verduin, Jr.. *Helping Students Develop investigative, Problem Solving, And Thinking Skills In A Cooperative Setting: A Handbook for Teachers, Administrators and Curriculum Workers* (Springfield, Illinois: Charles C. Thomas Publishers, 1996) and Dennis Adams and Mary Hamm, *Cooperative Learning: Critical Thinking and Collaboration Across the Curriculum* (Springfield: Illinois, Charles C. Thomas, Publisher, 1996).

3 Ibid., 4. See Neil Davidson and Toni Worshem, eds. *Enhancing Thinking Through Cooperative Learning* (N.Y. and London: Teachers College Press, 1992).

the course? For instance, in my Western Religions course I want my students to learn 1) how to read a text critically; 2) how to read a difficult text; 3) how to write clearly; 4) how to write a book review; and 5) how to revise and edit a short composition or essay. Write out expectations explicitly and include them in course objectives. Both you and your students will know exactly the task at hand. In fact, you will have a highly visible reminder of what you want to accomplish.

Instructors need constantly to evaluate their goals. For example, in teaching World Religions, is it really necessary to give students the grand survey of the major world religions, touching ever so lightly on all of the bases? Why not focus in depth on one Eastern Religion, one Western religion, and one other major religion, such as African religion, in which the class is particularly interested? Such an approach is appropriate particularly in those colleges and universities on the quarter, rather than the semester, system. In the quarter system, a class is typically taught for forty-six or forty-seven days. I teach World Religions five days a week. Despite that, I cannot do justice to all world religions in one quarter.

The same holds true for a History of Christianity course. Is it really possible to teach the development of Christianity from 100 C.E. to the present in a course that is taught three times a week for a little more than two months? Why not give an overview of the patristic age, the Middle Ages, the Reformation, the Victorian period, and the present? Then highlight a major thinker in each of those periods: Augustine, Aquinas, Luther, Newman, and Barth, for instance.

In sum, instructors should stop worrying about course coverage and ask themselves this question: How can students become independent, self-directed learners? One must teach students how to **learn**, how to **find information** on world religions and the history of Christianity, and how to be **reflective** about their own learning.

How does one teach students to be self-directed learners? For starters, demand that your students get an E-mail account at the computer center, if that is possible at your institution. Encourage your students to E-mail you with their questions and concerns about the course. If your class is small you may want to have part of an examination based on their ability to find information about religious studies on the Internet.

Faculty should make themselves practically superfluous so that students can take charge of their own learning, particularly in this era of information overload. That is one of the main goals of teaching critical thinking and one of the primary reasons for infusing critical thinking into the academic study of religion.

It is true that graduate students need to know a vast amount of information in order to pass their comprehensive examinations. However, professors can ask questions that test students' critical thinking abilities rather than merely test their recall abilities, as Chapter Nine of this book will illustrate.

In fact, I would argue that it is more important for students to think and to learn the methodology in the field of religious studies than it is to have arcane knowledge available to them at their fingertips. If enough professors of religion saw the benefits of teaching higher-order thinking skills and examined students for evidence of such abilities, the problem of making graduate education comprehensive would solve itself. *Solvitur ambulando.*

Barrier # 2: The Force of Habit

By and large faculty tend to teach as they were taught. In my own case that means the lecture method. The lecture method remains king of the hill in about 85 percent of the colleges and universities in this country. When candidates for a teaching position are asked to teach a model course to demonstrate their abilities, they are inclined to use the standard lecture format. In fact, they fear that using other methods will jeopardize their chances to land the job.

The lecture method can be very efficient, particularly in classes of a hundred or more students. It remains an excellent way of delivering information to a large number of students. However, lectures are not appropriate when the content is abstract, complex, or detailed or when students are asked to integrate the material with previous learning or life experience. Lectures work when product, rather than process, outcomes are paramount, but not when the instructional objective is getting students to think for themselves.

However, the straight lecture is not the only way to teach. In fact, lecture-based teaching, if used exclusively, is out-of-date, patterned as it is after the medieval collegiate model. Before Gutenberg's printing press, in the fifteenth century, professors dictated their notes to students because books had to be handwritten and their cost was prohibitive. Now what we have in too many courses in religious studies across the United States is all talk, all the time, with little application that touches students' lives. The use of the lecture exclusively is like listening to a Sunday sermon four hours a day for five days a week. No wonder our students may find higher education boring.[4]

Students who do well in such a system have excellent memories and are primarily aural learners. This is not to say that the material is retained. Memory works by association. We learn when we connect new

---

[4] David N. Campbell, "All Talk: Why Our Students Don't Learn," *Educational Horizons* 68 No. 1 (Fall, 1989), 3.

information to previous information or when a particular experience has meaning for us. We learn permanently when we integrate our knowledge into our existing understanding.[5]

Emphasis on teacher-centered learning puts students into a passive, dependent position. The instructor, not the student, is the active partner in the teaching-learning process. Critical thinking, on the other hand, tends to be student-centered. It transforms students into active learners.

Some faculty members have become accustomed to the straight lecture method and do not perceive its weaknesses. For instance, faculty assume, erroneously I believe, that students are listening to them most of the time. Additionally, the message sent is not always the message received. In my experience students frequently have pre-existing opinions about the material I deliver. These opinions, whether supported by evidence or not, can distort the instructional message. Because many opinions are unarticulated, and sometimes even unrecognized by the students themselves, this only intensifies their power to interfere with learning.

Teaching Thinking
In teaching students about religion I am simultaneously teaching them about thinking, that is, about using their minds for specific tasks. The academic study of religion, says Jacob Neusner, teaches students three things: (1) sustained analysis, (2) logical thinking, and (3) how to write a composition someone else will want to read.[6]

A scholar re-thinks what everyone automatically assumes to be the case. In a system that strives to create scholars, it is more important that students learn than that faculty teach. When students get excited about the study of religion, it is important not that the material is covered but that the excitement is kept alive.

We are creatures of habit. We accept the conventional wisdom that says that professors are expected to lecture. And change is always threatening. Hence some faculty say, "I don't want to make waves by trying out the newest teaching fads. I'd prefer to go with the tried and true. Besides, I already have my lecture notes neatly laid out." It is easy to become comfortable with the lecture method or any other *status quo*. But

---

[5] Charles C. Bonwell and James A. Eison, *Active Learning: Creating Excitement in the Classroom. ASHE-ERIC Higher Education Report No. 1* (Washington, D. C.: The George Washington University, 1991), 4. Active learning assumes that learning is by nature an active exercise and that different people learn in different ways. See Chet Meyers and Thomas B. Jones, *Promoting Active Learning: Strategies for the College Classroom* (San Francisco: Jossey-Bass Publishers, 1993).

[6] Jacob Neusner, *How To Grade Your Professors* (Boston: Beacon Press, 1984), 90.

we must ask which teaching method works best. What techniques are optimal in helping students learn and become independent thinkers? The answer is to use a variety of teaching methods. To depend on only one method is to be self-limiting.

Barrier # 3: The Fear of Failure

Professors who use critical thinking in the academic study of religion typically face at least two risks: the risk of engaging in new behavior (which will be judged critically by peers) and the risk of how students will, in fact, react to critical thinking.[7]

Often an instructor's feeling that "they won't let me innovate" is just a myth. Few faculty know or care what their peers do behind the closed doors of the classroom. In fact, a new teacher's star might rise if he or she successfully infuses critical thinking into the academic study of religion. Peers might then sing one's pedagogical praises. Additionally, student evaluations conceivably could be much better than if one lectured all the time. One thing is certain: I feel great satisfaction when I can get students actively involved in their own education by making use of higher-order thinking skills in the classroom.

Student Reaction

How will students react to the introduction of critical thinking into the religious studies curriculum? Much depends on how a particular instructor goes about the task. I find it helpful at the start of a course to introduce students to the ABCs of critical thinking. I spend two or three classes discussing the notion of critical thinking, explaining why it is important, and then giving students a couple of practical exercises in which they get a chance to use their knowledge of critical thinking in a real-life situation.

For example, I ask students to take out a piece of paper and jot down the answer to this question: How do you learn best? I then ask them to share their responses in small groups of three to five students. In each group I ask the members to appoint someone to record the flow of the conversation and to report back to the larger group. This exercise forces students to think while simultaneously encouraging them to be reflective about the teaching-learning process.

Using a Teaching Journal

The nervousness one feels as an instructor in trying out new teaching strategies is normal. But students tend to give the instructor the benefit

---

7 Bonwell and Eison, 62.

of the doubt when it comes to implementing new techniques. Once students see the rationale for the use of critical thinking in the academic study of religion, they feel quite comfortable with the new learning that inevitably takes place.

I use a notebook to record students' reactions to particular techniques and teaching strategies that I use. I then have a source to jog my memory about the pros and cons of using a particular strategy. Rather than being a hit-and-miss affair, teaching becomes a tried-and-true method based on controlled experimentation. And my teaching log becomes a valuable resource as I plan my next course.

Barrier # 4: The Problem of Definition

How is one to infuse critical thinking into the academic study of religion when educators cannot agree on a definition of critical thinking? Multiple and widely divergent definitions abound. Barry K. Beyer, for example, defines critical thinking as "the evaluation of statements, arguments and experiences" while Harvey Segal sees it as "thinking appropriately moved by reasons."[8]

These definitions are representative primarily in their differences. Beyer's definition is much more specific than Segal's. On the other hand, Segal's definition highlights the mind's tendency to be affected by things other than reason, such as emotion, punishment, and social reward, as Richard Paul observes.[9] A host of other critical-thinking definitions were discussed in depth in the previous chapter. But the existence of multiple definitions of critical thinking does not mean we are unable to infuse critical thinking into the academic study of religion. In fact, since we have many definitions of critical thinking, we are able to transcend the limitations of each.

Scholars in religious studies are accustomed to ambiguity. Hundreds of definitions of religion exist. Does this fact hinder scholarly research in religion? The answer is a resounding "no." Scholars also struggle with the relationship between religious studies and theological studies. Most faculty in public and private universities with graduate programs oppose the inclusion of theological studies in their programs, as Ray L. Hart observes in his lengthy study, "Religious and Theological Studies in American Higher Education."[10] I would argue that the same situation

---

8 Richard Paul, *Critical Thinking: What Every Person Needs to Survive in a Rapidly Changing World* (Rohnert Park, CA: Center for Critical Thinking and Moral Critique, 1990), 31.

9 Ibid.

10 Ray L. Hart, "Religious and Theological Studies in American Higher Education," *Journal of the American Academy of Religion* 59 No. 4, (1991), 715–827. In regard to the relationship between religion and critical thinking, see Jack Russell Weinstein, "Three Types of

applies to critical thinking. We do not need absolute clarity and agreement as to what constitutes critical thinking before infusing it into the academic study of religion.

Barrier # 5: Lack of Models

Instructors fear that devising strategies to promote critical thinking in the academic study of religion will be time-consuming. This barrier looms even larger when we consider that infusing critical thinking into the academic study of religion will require blazing new trails since little scholarly research has been done in the area. But the situation is not as bad as such statements would suggest. Critical thinking has been used successfully in many disciplines related to religious studies, such as philosophy and the social sciences, and analogues do exist.

The Rewards of Teaching for Critical Thinking

If we cannot avoid the fact that developing strategies for critical thinking will require effort, we can at least be assured that our work will be rewarding. I find that I am immeasurably enriched by teaching critical thinking. If I merely dispense information to students, I feel guilty. I feel that I have not given students what they need to become independent, self-directed learners.

Students may prefer highly structured work with one right answer, but if I do not teach procedural or how-to knowledge, I have not done an adequate job of teaching. The dividends are paramount in terms of student response. However tempting it is to take out last year's lecture notes, dust them off, update them in spots, and pass them off as the best that can be done, it is more important to empower students to learn and to think on their own rather than to parrot back what we have said. When our students blaze a trail of their own and go beyond the confines of convention, they pay us the highest compliment possible.

In trying to infuse critical thinking into the academic study of religion, you will be riding the wave of the future. Start small. Work on injecting critical thinking into a segment of one of your courses. For instance, take a small section of a course you are thoroughly familiar with and ask yourself this question: "How can I teach this aspect of the course in a way that emphasizes critical thinking?"

There are several tacks to take in answering this question. First, before discussing this topic in class one may ask students to write down what words they associate with the topic under consideration, say the term

Critical Thinking About Religion: A Response to William Reinsmith," *Inquiry: Critical Thinking Across the Disciplines*, Vol. XV, No. 3 (Spring, 1996) 79–88.

conscience in an Ethics course or the word *worship* in a course on Myth, Symbol, and Rite. One may then have the class divide into groups of three to discuss their responses.

Second, after giving a mini-lecture for fifteen minutes on conscience or the term *worship*, ask students to write down in their notebooks how this lecture pertains to their own lives. One cannot assume that students will see the connection between the course material and their own lives. One must **explicitly** ask students to make this connection. The connection may not be very obvious to students, hence this exercise forces them to think and to reflect on what they are learning.

Third, one may require students to write a critique of your lecture, noting positive and negative aspects of it. Then ask them to write a 200-word essay on the same topic if they were giving the mini-lecture. Students may then be put into small learning groups to share their individual essays. One may then have a large group discussion of the same topic. Once students have shared their ideas in small groups of four they will more likely feel confident enough to share their ideas with the entire class. I take it as axiomatic that the more you teach the same course, the more ideas you will have for infusing critical thinking into other segments of it.

Barrier # 6: The Evaluation of Critical Thinking

How is critical thinking and higher-order thinking—interpretation, analysis, or manipulation of information to answer a question that cannot be resolved using the routine application of previously learned knowledge—to be evaluated in ways that are compatible with current accountability systems? This is a pseudo-barrier. There are, indeed, various ways to evaluate a student's ability to think critically and creatively, to solve problems and to demonstrate higher-order thinking. Assessment agencies in California, Connecticut, Illinois, Michigan, New Jersey, New York, and Vermont are currently developing alternative measures. We also have the Cornell Critical Thinking Tests, Level X and Level Z, and the Ennis-Weir Critical Thinking Essay Test.[11]

---

[11] Ernest McDaniel and Chris Lawrence, *Levels of Cognitive Complexity: An Approach to the Measurement of Thinking* (New York: Springer-Verlag, 1990), 5. In both forms, students identify instances of good versus bad reasoning by evaluating statements. Students construct a response to arguments by writing a "letter to the editor" in the Ennis-Weir Critical Thinking Essay Test. See Elizabeth A. Jones, ed., *et al, National Assessment of College Student Learning: Identifying College Graduates' Essential Skills in Writing, Speech and Listening, and Critical Thinking: Final Project Report* (Washington, D.C.: U.S. Department of Education: Office of Educational Research and Improvement, 1995). This study tries to reach a consensus among a group of faculty, employers, and policymakers, on the specific higher

Essay exams are an easy way of assessing students' ability to think critically and creatively, but it is also possible to devise multiple choice exams that test for higher-order thinking. For instance, after students are instructed to circle the response to a multiple-choice question, I ask them to provide a one-sentence reason for their selection. Their answers reveal much about their reasoning processes—and force them to think about those processes.

Barrier # 7: No Incentive to Change

Faculty often have no incentive to change their teaching approach. Most faculty are hired on the basis of their expertise in their discipline and only secondarily on the basis of their teaching ability. The majority of faculty were not introduced to teaching as a discipline with its own research agenda, professional organizations, and journals. Nor were many faculty required to take courses in education and pedagogy before they were sent into the classroom as graduate teaching assistants. In professional schools faculty are prone to offer their knowledge on a "take it or leave it" basis and hence are not receptive to developing their teaching skills.

The reward system at most academic institutions favors those who publish and, at least in research universities, bring in big research dollars. Ten years ago I gave a presentation on creative teaching to an audience consisting mainly of university professors. One of the professors stood up and said, "Why are you telling us to be creative teachers? We're not going to be rewarded for our teaching but for our research and ability to attract large grant money." I had to admit to myself that this professor was correct. The present reward system is not geared to rewarding teaching, yet even that is changing.

I find that the pendulum even at large research universities is now swinging away from research with a concomitant emphasis on quality teaching. Part of the momentum for this swing has to do with the renewed stress on assessment and evaluation. In some states the legislature wants to see that the money earmarked for higher education is well-spent and that administrators are held accountable for how well students at public institutions do on standardized tests such as the Graduate Record Examination.

Administrators at the Dean's level and above are concerned with quality teaching. Thus faculty must demonstrate that they are good teachers as measured by student evaluations, peer evaluations, and the perusal of syllabi when faculty are up for promotion and/or tenure. It

---

order communication/thinking skills that college graduates should achieve to become effective employees in the workplace and citizens in society.

no longer suffices to be a first-rate researcher. One's teaching must also be of the first-order if one is to gain tenure even at major research universities in this country.

Barrier # 8: A Diverse Student Body

Faculty in religion have fewer well-prepared students than they did even twenty years ago. The proportion and number of eighteen- to twenty-two-year-old students from lower economic and social strata have increased significantly. Secondary schools, particularly in urban areas have experienced a continual decline in standards, leaving many colleges with a large number of at-risk students. In the past twenty years the number of African-American, Hispanic-American, and Asian-American students has increased. They bring to college their own goals, histories, and values, which differ greatly from those of the traditional undergraduate. Changing immigration patterns have also resulted in more and more students with limited proficiency in English.

The almost spectacular rise in the number of returning adult students is also part of the equation. Many adults are returning to school in hopes of entering fields where jobs are available. They are a very diverse group, from well-prepared students pursuing a career change to those burdened with family/economic responsibilities to those marginally equipped for college.

As Stetar and Jemmott point out, these developments have transformed college classrooms into a patchwork of diverse student academic skills, aptitudes, attitudes, backgrounds, and interests.[12] One cannot simply present material and presume that students will master it. Some faculty, frustrated with the numbers of unprepared students in their classrooms, simply write off today's students as either inferior or unteachable. These faculty constantly lecture their peers about how incompetent students are today, how they are unable to write coherent English, how they cannot think for themselves, and the like.

Some academics, perhaps far removed from their own student days, have unrealistic expectations for students. Is it reasonable for professors of religion to expect beginning students to read Tillich's *Systematic Theology*? Part of the job of teaching religion is instructing students in how to read a difficult text. A distinction needs to be drawn between what students are expected to bring to the academic study of religion and what they are expected to develop while studying religion. Similarly, we may distinguish between an entry failing and an exit failing.

---

[12] Joseph M. Stetar and Nina Dorset Jemmott, "Fostering Faculty: Institutional Loyalty and Professional Rewards," *The Review of Higher Education* (Winter, 1991) 14, No. 2, 265.

Teaching Skills

The changing demographics of higher education argue that critical thinking is needed today more than ever. A knowledge of religion may not translate immediately into a specific job for the majority of students, but if studying religion teaches students how to ask intelligent questions, how to express themselves clearly and accurately, and how to think then its value is ensured. As Jacob Neusner shrewdly observes, intellectual skills cannot be taken from us. Whatever technical skill one gains for a specific career will be hollow without the ability to think critically.[13]

Some educators maintain that disciplined or critical thinking does not occur in classrooms because students today do not have the intelligence required for higher-order thinking. The bell-shaped curve of intelligence distribution suggests that only a small percentage of students will be able to engage in higher-order thinking. Although some educators maintain that instruction in thinking is inappropriate for low-achieving students, other educators argue that such skills as creating analogies and restructuring can be taught successfully to less proficient students. In order to bring this off successfully two things must be done: 1) teachers must have adequate instruction in coaching, guided practice, and modeling, and 2) students must be given help in both cognitive and metacognitive strategies. Evidence exists that creativity, intelligence, and talent are not scarce resources but are, in fact, almost without limit. Virtually all students can learn whatever they are motivated to learn.[14]

Barrier # 9: Lack of Imagination

Have you ever muttered to yourself, "My colleagues are creative, not me." It is easy to take a defeatist attitude about one's teaching, but we can develop our creativity. We must first acknowledge the way things are, including whatever appears dark and foreboding. Then we must envision what we hope to create. This does not mean that we must change ourselves: we simply have to face the obstacles with inner strength and use our imagination to slip around them.

For example, each class has its own personality. Just as individuals may be overbearing and hard to take, so too may entire classes. I once taught a class in which a negative atmosphere developed: the students

---

[13] Jacob Neusner, 90.

[14] Rexford Brown, *Schools of Thought: How the Politics of Literacy Shape Thinking in the Classroom* (San Francisco: Jossey-Bass Publishers, 1991), 241. Attitude or motivation is a key component of a critical thinker. See the discussion in Diane Halpern, *Thought and Knowledge: An Introduction to Critical Thinking*, Third Edition. (Mahwah, New Jersey: Lawrence Erlbaum Associates, Publishers, 1996) 25.

did not like one another, and at least three different cliques kept the class from coming together as a group. Finding the class increasingly difficult, I dreaded walking into the room. One day I decided to address the problem head-on. I told students that the atmosphere in this class needed a change, and we then used brainstorming to suggest some possible changes. We would hear any idea, no matter how wild. We wound up with ten good ideas for changing the atmosphere in the class, including forming discussion groups so that each interest group in the class could express its concerns. The changes that resulted were quite dramatic. I started looking forward to the class sessions, and students now said how much they enjoyed the class.

Barrier # 10: Issues of Power and Authority

Professors are accustomed to having the respect of students. As the ultimate authority in the classroom, they make decisions about what will be learned and how. And they have the power to influence their students' lives even beyond the classroom: they dole out the grades. The veteran student knows only too well the rules of the game: take careful and extensive notes, never challenge the professor directly, give back on exams the professor's own opinion on the subject, and never be antagonistic in the classroom. In short, do whatever it takes to pass the course. This particular apple cart may be upset if professors abandon their traditional roles in the classroom and become seekers of knowledge and midwives or coaches in the teaching-learning situation. Everyone benefits from these changes: the professor who is reinvigorated in his or her teaching and the students who gain useful, empowering skills that will serve them in whatever they do.

Summary

In this chapter we have examined some of the most important barriers to introducing critical thinking into the academic study of religion.[15] These barriers, though real, are not insurmountable. In the next chapter

---

[15] The goal of education in the United States needs to be re-thought. Presently, the goal is to give students the facts and basic skills they will need in order to be successful in life. Our textbooks, teaching styles and evaluation of the teaching/learning process reflect this vision. Students of religious studies will not become more thoughtful unless the improvement of thinking becomes the basic goal of higher education. See Patricia A. McGrane and Robert J. Sternberg, "Discussion: Fatal Vision—The Failure of the Schools in Teaching Children to Think," in *Teaching Thinking: An Agenda for the Twenty-First Century* eds. Cathy Collins and John N. Mangieri (Hillsdale, N.J.: Lawrence Erlbaum Associates, 1992), 333.

we will take a look at the three levels of learning. The first level deals with declarative knowledge or the "facts" level. The second level examines procedural knowledge, which is also known as the "skills" level and the third level has to do with metacognition, or "thinking about one's thinking."

3

The Three Levels of Learning

"What one knows is, in youth, of little moment, they know enough who know how to learn."

Henry Adams

In the previous chapter we discussed several barriers to critical thinking. This chapter concerns itself with learning, in general, understood as the process whereby novices become more expert in a particular knowledge domain and, in particular, the three levels of learning: 1) declarative knowledge, which includes concepts, facts, principles, stories, and other propositional knowledge that is used to make inferences; 2) strategic or procedural knowledge, or the skills required to drive a car, do multiplication, write a book review, or find information in the library; and 3) metacognition, or thinking about thinking, which involves such control strategies as making plans, asking questions, setting goals, taking notes, observing the effectiveness of one's efforts, and taking corrective action.

Critical thinking concerns all three levels of learning which form an organic whole but which can be separated and looked at in isolation from each other for purposes of analysis. In other words, critical thinking deals with all three levels of learning: declarative knowledge, procedural knowledge, and metacognition. I would argue that most faculty in the humanities, in general, and religious studies, in particular, concern themselves mainly with declarative knowledge so that higher-order thinking is given short shrift. For this reason most of this chapter deals with the skills students of religious studies need in order to be life-long, independent learners.

Declarative Knowledge: The First Level

The first level of learning, declarative knowledge, is sometimes referred to as lower-order thinking, in contradistinction to strategic or procedural knowledge and metacognition, which are termed higher-order thinking. Lower-order thinking occurs when learners are asked to receive factual information or to use rules and algorithms through repetitive routines.

Higher-order thinking, on the other hand, requires learners to manipulate information and ideas in ways that transform their meaning. The phrase *lower-order thinking* should not be thought of as pejorative. Students must know basic terms of religion before they can be literate in the field of religious studies, just as they must know some basic concepts and principles in physics before they can be scientifically literate. One cannot teach students higher-order thinking skills and metacognition independent of specific knowledge about religion. Indeed, the process of teaching students how to think is a complex network of relations among declarative knowledge, skills, and metacognition.[1]

Cultural Literacy

E. D. Hirsch, Jr., speaks of cultural literacy, or the network of information that all competent readers possess.[2] Cultural literacy refers, then, to background information stored in our memories that allows us to read and comprehend an article and relate it to the unstated context, which gives meaning to what is read. In other words, one must know a great deal that is not set down explicitly on the page in order to grasp the meaning of an article.

In an Introduction to Religion course, students should know certain key terms and their definitions: religion, theology, philosophy, myth, parable, metaphor, symbol, sign, sacrament, mystery, eschatology, ecclesiology, hermeneutics, exegesis, and phenomenology, for instance. However, it is very easy to become so caught up with teaching basic terms and concepts that other levels of learning are ignored. The result is that too much lecturing takes place in our courses in religious studies on both the undergraduate and graduate levels, leading to too much emphasis on rote memorization and too little application that has meaning to students. Most classrooms are basically the same: rows of desks face a professor who lectures to passive, note-taking students.

---

1 Grace E. Grant, *Teaching Critical Thinking* (New York: Praeger, 1988), 6. See Alison King, "Inquiry as a Tool in Critical Thinking," *Changing College Classrooms: New Teaching and Learning Strategies for an Increasingly Complex World* Diane F. Halpern and Associates, eds. (San Francisco: Jossey-Bass Publishers, 1994), 13–38; and Brenda H. Manning and Beverly D. Payne, *Self-talk for Teachers and Students: Metacognitive Strategies for Personal and Classroom Use* (Boston: Allyn and Bacon, 1995).

2 E. D. Hirsch, Jr., *Cultural Literacy: What Every American Needs to Know* (Boston: H. Mifflin Co., 1987), 2. One reason why students often have difficulty with the textbooks we choose is their lack of the "cultural literacy" assumed by the text's author, i.e., students do not have access to the cultural codes of the text (background, common knowledge, allusions) that the author assumed that the reader would know. See John C. Bean, *Engaging Ideas: The Professor's Guide to Integrating Writing, Critical Thinking, and Active Learning in the Classroom* (San Francisco: Jossey-Bass Publishers, 1996) 136.

The Problem of Textbooks

Who or what is to blame for this lamentable situation? Both professors and their textbooks. As we discussed in the previous chapter, professors are conditioned to teach as they were taught. Many do not know any other way. Textbooks largely define the content of what is taught in our universities. U.S. textbooks are unrivaled in size and in the amount of information they cover. A popular textbook for World Religions courses contains 700 pages. Those who teach on the quarter system need to cover thirty pages every class day in order to cover the material in the book before the term ends. Information overload is not limited to religious studies. Science textbooks in the United States are, for instance, considerably larger than their counterparts in Japan and Singapore, where students have higher achievement test scores than do our students.

Because our textbooks are so weighty, professors are forced to teach for exposure. Students receive a superficial introduction to a large amount of information, and the real point of the class is often lost. Less content taught more effectively over successive years will lead to greater religious literacy for our students.

Throwaway Knowledge

In "The Quality School Curriculum," William Glasser speaks of "throwaway knowledge."[3] He uses this term to describe facts one must know in order to pass a test, afterwards to be thrown away. Dates and places in the history of Christianity, divisions of religious studies, and statistics on the number of adherents of a particular religion are all examples of throwaway knowledge. Instead of fixating on the "throwaway knowledge" of religion as an end in itself, we need to pay attention to two other forms of knowledge, strategic knowledge and metacognition.

Strategic or Procedural Knowledge: The Second Level

Procedural or strategic knowledge employs declarative knowledge to execute a skilled performance. Strategic knowledge describes the skills required to accomplish specific tasks: write a book review, drive a car, or find information in the library. Procedural knowledge deals with skills understood as the ability to do something well, arising from talent, training, or practice. Procedural knowledge is rarely taught because for most professors it functions as tacit knowledge, which is implicit and unformulated.

[3] William Glasser, "The Quality School Curriculum," *Phi Delta Kappan* 73 no. 9 (May 1992): 690.

Instead of worrying about covering the material, we need to concentrate on the priority of skills our students in religion need to handle the course content by themselves. Professors must think through the kinds of skills students need in order to become progressively less dependent on their teachers. Consider the implications of writing a term paper. Teachers and textbooks talk about writing as though it were a subject rather than a process. Students, however, must learn the process by which they can create the product; that is, they must master the basic tools of writing.

What Is a Skill?

A skill, then, may be defined as the ability to use knowledge. What skills should our students possess? And how are they to acquire, retrieve, and retain them? In order to answer the first question we will briefly explore five skills that relate to "getting ready to learn." They are self-evaluation, goal setting, time management, monitoring attitudes, and motivation.[4]

1) Self-Evaluation.   Self-evaluation is the ability to assess learning skills that students may (or may not) possess. Self-evaluation answers the question, "What skills do I need to learn?" Researchers suggest two criteria for self-evaluation: 1) reflection on previous learning experiences and 2) motivation for learning how to learn.[5]

At least three benefits are associated with the assessment of one's learning style: 1) students will develop a balanced approach to learning; 2) they will capitalize on their strong suit in terms of their learning preference and improve upon their deficits; and 3) they will discover their personal preferences for developing skills and acquiring information.

To facilitate self-evaluation and assessment, ask students to reflect on their experience of learning. I usually ask my students to write or talk about several experiences where they were very satisfied with the learning product or process. Students can create a list of strengths and weaknesses by identifying specific skills and feelings connected with the learning.

---

[4] Joanne McKay and Janey Montgomery, *A Guide to Developing Learning Across the Curriculum* (Des Moines, Iowa: Iowa Department of Education, 1990), 17. I am indebted to McKay and Montgomery for most of this section. In the psychology of religion a key skill would be critically evaluating a source. See James Bell, *Evaluating Psychological Information: Sharpening Your Critical Thinking Skills* Second Edition, (Boston: Allyn and Bacon, 1995); Robert J. Sternberg and Louise Spear-Swerling, *Teaching for Thinking* (Washington, D.C.: American Psychological Association, 1996), 55–64; Marcia Heiman and Joshua Slomianko, eds. *Thinking Skills Instruction: Concepts and Techniques* (Washington, D.C.: National Education Association, 1987) and Karen Scheid, *Helping Students Become Strategic Learners: Guidelines for Teaching* (Cambridge, MA: Brookline Books, 1993), 21–45.

[5] Ibid., 20

For example, I began a seminar in religion by asking students to write 300 words on their best learning experience and their worst. I then asked them to reflect on what made the best learning experience such a good one and why did they have such negative feelings about their worst learning experience. They then discussed in a small group their positive and negative learning experiences. A large group was then formed in which students answered this question: What could you have done to turn your negative learning experiences into positive ones?

How does the notion of self-motivation relate to the academic study of religion? For in-class presentations, have students develop criteria that can be used to judge the project. Then set standards by assigning levels of proficiency. A 1-to-10 scale on labels such as "strongly agree" or "strongly disagree" could be used.[6] In a World Religions course, students may develop a pictorial dictionary that serves as a glossary of foreign words they have mastered. Pictures may be used from a variety of sources to illustrate common vocabulary in the various religions.

2) Goal setting. Goal setting involves identifying a destination and then developing a plan to get there. Goal setting increases the likelihood that a task will be completed, enhances the probability of student success, and helps students learn from their failures. Skills subsumed under the general category of goal setting include 1) stating the goal in writing, 2) setting a time frame in which to reach the goal, 3) imagining reaching the goal, 4) writing an action plan to reach the goal, 5) identifying the next steps toward accomplishing the goal, 6) estimating the time needed to complete each step of the plan, and 7) evaluating the relationship between the goal and the action plan.

Goal setting may be used at the beginning of a class period for a specific subject or task, when students have a strong desire to attain a particular goal or when students want to systematically attack an issue. Goals may be one of two types: long term or short term. In a language course on Biblical Greek, ask each student to set a long-term goal for self-improvement in the language. The teacher may ask students to determine what is needed to be more fluent in the language and have them write the steps, figure out the time needed to meet the goal, and set a target date for accomplishing it.

One may also ask students to set short-term goals. Begin the class by telling students what the learning objectives are for the day and then ask them to determine a short-range goal for today's class. For example, by the end of today's class in Biblical Greek I will be able to tell the difference between the first and the second aorist indicative.

[6] Ibid., 45.

Goal setting may be a valuable skill for professors who run internship programs for religion majors. Whether directing a religious education program in a parish, doing counseling work in a hospital or prison, or organizing and running a thrift shop, students will set goals, plan the project, and see it to completion. Having a plan that arises from goal setting allows both the professor and the intern to know what needs to be accomplished when and provides a structure against which performance can be evaluated.

3) Time management.   Time management is a skill students use to determine how well they are using their time. It includes scheduling time, evaluating the use of time, and exploring changes in the management of time.

Pacing, or estimating how long it will take to complete an activity, is a key element in time management. Students become aware of their own learning pace through trial and error, but the A.B.C. method of prioritizing can help them estimate blocks of time needed for a project. "A" stands for something that one must do today, "B" for something important that could be done tomorrow or next week, and "C" for something that could be postponed.

Time management is essential in doing a saturation research paper or a term paper. I have students place tasks on a calendar with a specific date for completion, allotting time for researching and writing components of the paper. Two weeks into the class I want to know the name and direction of the research paper; at four weeks I want to see the notes taken. After six weeks I demand a first draft, and after eight weeks I ask for the final copy. Many of my students have difficulty meeting the target date for the final copy unless they meet interim dates while the paper is in process.

4) Monitoring attitudes.   Four key elements affect students' rate of learning and retention: 1) the level of distraction, 2) attitude toward the value of instruction, 3) attitude about work, and 4) attitude toward succeeding. Monitoring attitudes requires attention control and power thinking.

Attention control, or monitoring and consciously controlling one's attention level, is a key ingredient to doing well on any task. It may be used to highlight important information and to get students to pay attention to a task they do not like. Energy control, bracketing, and power thinking are methods of attention enhancement. Energy control means raising or lowering one's energy at will, e.g., using relaxation exercises to overcome test anxiety. Bracketing, on the other hand, puts aside thoughts that are irrelevant to the task at hand. Power thinking refers to the conscious control of thinking through positive self-statements.[7] Power thinking is effective in preparing for some difficult task. One may gain insight into power thinking by considering its opposite: self-doubt. Students who doubt themselves will often refuse to study and learn, or they will procrastinate in completing assignments. In teaching Religion in America or Eastern Religions have students identify the attitudes of men and women who colonized the United States, founded a religion, or left the east to go to the west. Ask students how the attitudes and behaviors of those who discovered new frontiers differ from those who elected to stay home. Analyzing these qualities will give students both insight and examples to emulate.

5) Motivation.   There are two types of motivation: intrinsic and extrinsic. Intrinsic motivation comes from within the learner and includes such items as pleasure, power, and satisfaction from accomplishing objectives. Extrinsic motivation involves some goal, incentive, or reward extrinsic to the task. Several factors influence the motivation of students: classroom environment, empowerment, instructional strategies, rewards, and student success. In general, the learner's needs generate motivation, which may be seen as the force that guides a person's actions.

How does the skill of motivation apply to the classroom situation? Have students look at the founders of Buddhism, Confucianism, and Christianity in order to determine what motivated them and what or who influenced them. Look at the lives of saints in the Hindu, Buddhist, and Taoist religious traditions. What motivated these saints to devote their lives to a cause or a particular god? Have students study a career in religion such as pastor, spiritual director, teacher of religious education, marriage counselor, or editor of books in religion. They can job shadow an individual in the career they have chosen and interview that person about his or her motivation and self-concept. Students can determine what motivated their subjects at the beginning of their careers and what inspires them now.

Finally, ask students to write down what motivates them and then practice strategies designed to heighten both intrinsic and extrinsic motivation. Invite individuals working in the area of religious studies or graduate students to meet with undergraduates. Have them talk about what they do in their vocation and what motivates them. In this way students will understand the concept of motivation and why it helps people make career choices.

---

[7] Ibid., 23.

As students develop and enhance their skills in time management, goal setting, and evaluation, they need to learn about and gain experience in five other skill areas.

1) Locating information in religious studies.   Students should be able to identify and use reference tools, including major encyclopedias (*The Encyclopedia of Religion*, *Encyclopedia Judaica*, etc.) and electronic databases such as the c.d. rom in the Humanities. They should also be able to locate and use bibliographies and newspaper indexes, as well as such specialized reference sources as *The Humanities* Index, *The Catholic Periodical Index*, and *Religion Index One: Periodicals*. Finally, in addition to being able to operate microfiche and film readers and printers and photocopy machines, they should know how to identify services and materials provided by information networks and electronic databases.

One of the best ways to teach students the resources of the library is to build a library session into the structure of the course. At the start of the term set up a library tour in the area of religious studies with the bibliographic librarian. This should be a hands-on session in which students actually sit down at the computer and learn how to use the c.d. rom. To make sure that students attend these sessions, tell them ahead of time that the material covered in this library session will be on the midterm examination.

2) Selecting information in religious studies.   Students should be able to distinguish between fact and opinion in books and journal articles dealing with religious studies. Facts have a verifiable truth value. I know that China has more than one billion people because I can point to reliable government surveys that say so. An opinion, on the other hand, is the simple assertion of a preference. To assert that Hinduism is the best religion in the world would be an opinion. Naked facts, untainted by opinion, are hard to find. One way to help students see the difference between fact and opinion is to have them carefully examine their textbook. Although authors of textbooks do not deliberately set out to mislead students, the facts that they report are often subject to interpretation. Word choice, the amount of information included, and the events included or omitted all contribute to the "factual" information that is printed.[8]

It is important to help students recognize trends and patterns on a given topic over time. One way to help students do this is to have them carefully examine a journal such as *The Journal for the Scientific Study of Religion* for articles on, say, fundamentalism, over a twenty-year period.

---

[8] Diane F. Halpern, *Thought and Knowledge: An Introduction to Critical Thinking* Third Edition (Mahwah: New Jersey: Lawrence Erlbaum Associates, Publishers, 1996), 201–203.

What trends emerge over such a span of time? What do the articles have in common? What structural features are the same or different?

Students must also be taught how to recognize supportive detail and make inferences. An inference is the same as a deduction. It is the act of passing from one or more statements considered as true to another, the truth of which is believed to follow from that of the former. For example, consider this simple story:

> Mary inherited a large sum of money. John loves racing cars and living high. John married Mary.

This is a meaningful story, although it provides little factual information. A reader may infer that John married Mary for her money, which he will use to buy racing cars and live well. Comprehension often requires the reader to make inferences by going beyond the words uttered. One may say one thing verbally while implying something quite different. Advertisers often use this technique to persuade their audiences to buy products but stay within the legal restrictions on the kinds of statements they can make.

A distinction must be drawn between factual beliefs, which can be verified by direct observation, and inferential beliefs, which go beyond what one can directly observe. I was recently stopped by the police because they suspected me of drunk driving. I had gone over the yellow line twice while driving at night and my wife and daughter were with me. I explained to the police officer that (a) I do not drink, (b) that the vehicle behind me was tailgating so closely that I was unable to see very clearly, and (c) that my vision is twenty over eight thousand. In other words what others can see eight thousand feet away I need to be twenty feet close to see.

The officer inferred that I was driving while drunk because I crossed the yellow line twice. After listening to my explanation the officer knew that his inference was wrong. He did not even bother to see if I could walk a straight line or take a breath analysis test. We make inferences all the time, and sometimes we have difficulty in drawing a hard and fast line between what is observed and what is inferred.[9] As teachers of religion one of our main tasks involves coming up with strategies by which students will learn for themselves what it means to be specific in writing a term paper. Once they have learned to be specific, students must then learn how to take a point of view toward the specifics that they have collected. Students must ask themselves such questions as "What do I think about these facts?" "Who is my audience?" "What do I want this term paper to do, analyze, inspire, or persuade?"

[9] John Chaffee, *Thinking Critically* (Boston: Houghton Mifflin, 1985), 394.

3) Organizing information in religious studies. The ability to organize information in religious studies, or any other field, requires several skills: a) the ability to create the basic skeletal form of an outline and to use an outline in both oral and written presentations; b) the ability to take effective notes and to use them to summarize information; c) and the ability to use study guides as a means of structuring individual reading.

The importance of taking good notes should not be underestimated. To take effective notes one must listen in a discriminating way; that is, one must distinguish essential from nonessential information. Note taking reveals the underlying structure of a lesson, enhances memory, and provides a written record of important information. Good notes are organized, complete, and contain the important parts or heart of the lecture. I find that the best students are those who take the best notes.

Organizing information effectively requires a number of skills, including the ability to classify patterns and techniques and identify main ideas, themes, and topics, as opposed to details. These skills should be introduced and nurtured as early as elementary school. In teaching undergraduates to read theologians like Rahner, Bultmann, and Pannenberg, I have them outline a particularly difficult chapter. It is a learning experience for students to come to terms with a heady thinker themselves rather than relying on my explanation. Students gain confidence that they can handle a difficult text if I explain to them the technical terms in a chapter, especially foreign words like *Weltanschauung, sola Scriptura*, and the difference between *Geschichte* and *Historie*.

4) Communicating information. Four basic skills—reading, writing, speaking, and listening—are essential in learning to learn. Using media is a fifth skill, but it is really a refined version of the basic four. Reading skills in religious studies involve vocabulary, comprehension, and reading-related study skills. The work of Nelson-Herber (1986) suggests that new vocabulary words should be taught in concept clusters. For example, when speaking of God's transcendence, I like to mention the opposite of transcendence, namely, the word *immanence*. Or, in speaking of the sacred, I will also mention its opposite, viz., the word *profane*.

To facilitate organization in meaning, vocabulary should be related to a student's prior knowledge.[10] One may do this by using two bridging strategies, **metaphors** and **advance organizers**. An advance organizer is a brief paragraph that comes before a lesson or unit of instruction. It is based on students' prior knowledge and makes a powerful transition statement. Advance organizers outline, arrange, and logically sequence

---

[10] See Janey L. Montgomery and Joanne W. McKay, "Learning to Learn Skills," in *Critical Thinking: Implications for Teaching and Teachers*, eds. Wendy Oxman and others (Montclair, New Jersey: Institute for Critical Thinking, 1992), 281.

the main points or ideas, providing students with a structure of the new information. The introduction to this chapter contains an advance organizer.

A **metaphor** is a figure of speech that is rich in imagery. Metaphors emphasize subtle, connotative meaning and consist of figurative language. For instance, this statement is a metaphor: "The glacier is flowing potato pancake batter."

One may view a metaphor as a word or phrase used inappropriately, i.e., it belongs properly in one context but is being used in another. For example, to speak of the "arm of a chair." A chair really has no anatomical parts since it is an inanimate object. One may also speak of chess as a "war game." Chess has some similarities to war; both involve opponents trying to gain the victory over one another. However, chess does not involve death, suffering, and violence the way war does.

How does a metaphor function as a bridging strategy? In using a metaphor it may be that relatively large portions of information (similarities) may be juxtaposed from prior knowledge to a new area of knowledge. For example, one may speak of Auburn University as a family. All the qualities associated with family, such as intimacy, caring, closeness, concern, are then carried over to Auburn University by using the metaphor of family.

One may divide reading-related study skills into prereading, reading, and proofreading. Prereading activities include giving students an overview of a difficult chapter and explaining new and complex concepts in advance. Before students tackle Karl Rahner's essay "Nature and Grace," for instance, I give them the scholastic definitions of the terms *nature* and *grace*.

During reading activities have students ask questions of the text, noting personal responses. Ask students what questions still remain after reading the chapter, which sections were the most difficult, and why this was the case. After they read the text, have students determine its main points. Ask students to rewrite those points for a reader who understands little or no theology.

Writing skills are covered elsewhere, but I do want to briefly mention media (understood as materials used to transmit information, e.g., books, pamphlets, films, video cassettes, cd roms, and computer programs) because they can be a powerful tool in the instructional process. There are several reasons media should be used: 1) to broaden communication skills, 2) to reinforce language skills, 3) to promote cultural understanding, 4) to help students respond to adult reality, and 5) to prepare students for employment.[11] For instance, I have used media such

[11] Joanne McKay and Janey Montgomery, *A Guide*, 29.

as films and slides to promote cultural understanding as I introduce students to Eastern religions.

A brief word needs to be said about **speaking** and **listening**. Speaking refers to language in action. The discipline known as speech includes voice and diction, rhetorical and communication theory, interpersonal communication, organizational communication, public speaking, mass media, oral interpretation, and argumentation and debate.

There are five communicative functions for speech. They are: 1) the expression of feelings, 2) ritual, 3) imagination, 4) the giving of information, and 5) persuasive discourse. Students of speech also learn audience analysis and examine the medium chosen by the speaker as the most effective in conveying the message from the sender to the receiver.

Listening

Listening is one of the four basic modes of communication. It is a process that includes attending, assigning meaning, discriminating, evaluating, perceiving, remembering, and responding. Listening should be taught in the classroom as part of the skills students need in order for cooperative learning to take place. As such, it will be discussed in this book later on in the chapter on cooperative learning.

5) Developing memory skills.   Memory training employs specific skills to increase the brain's capacity to remember, retain, and retrieve information.[12] One may use "deep processing" to highlight information in order to stimulate thought or memorize data. It helps one consciously generate emotions, linguistic information, mental images, and sensations about a thought, concept, or body of information. For instance, to deep process information about Jerusalem during a New Testament class, have students form a strong mental image of a city on a hill with lots of rocky streets. Ask them to picture the Old City, still surrounded by a massive torn wall and distinguished by its many churches and mosques. Suggest that they smell the scent of Oriental cooking and spices and hear the peal of church bells, the calls of muezzins from minarets, and the chanting of Jews praying at the Wailing Wall. What would the countryside look like? Rolling mountains with cedar trees or dry, barren desert? This combination of feelings, imagery, and information stimulates retention rates and promotes depth of processing. In short, deep processing generates verbal information and images, physical sensations, and feelings about that information.

12 Ibid., 29.

Metacognition: The Third Level

The term *metacognition* came into use around 1975. It grew out of orthodox Piagetian developmental theory. From its inception the term has been denounced as faddish and fuzzy, yet it has endured. Metacognition refers to one's knowledge and control of one's own cognitive system. One primary problem with the word is distinguishing between what is "meta" and what is "cognitive." For example, asking yourself questions about a chapter might function either to improve your knowledge (a cognitive function)[13] or to monitor it (a metacognitive function). Metacognition is a wide term and is very complex. In this chapter metacognition refers to such control strategies as making plans, setting goals, asking questions, taking notes, observing the effectiveness of one's efforts, and taking corrective action.[14] Expert thinkers not only use appropriate operations or large-scale strategies, but they also reflect on what they are doing; that is, they monitor themselves to stay on track. They also plan in advance and reflect afterwards to discover ways they might improve their thinking.[15]

Dispositions of Thoughtfulness
Some researchers use the terms *metacognition* and *dispositions of thoughtfulness* as synonyms. The latter term involves attitudes, personality, or character traits and general values and beliefs about the nature of knowledge. Dispositions of thoughtfulness involve a desire that claims be supported by reasons. In religious studies, for example, a theist may believe that the ontological proof for God's existence is valid. The claims of the theist are as strong as the arguments adduced in support of the conclusion. Thoughtfulness is characterized by a tendency to be reflective or to take time to think problems through for oneself. In regard to interreligious dialogue, for example, one may ask whether and how is it possible to affirm the validity of one's own religious tradition while also allowing for the possible validity of other religious traditions.[16]

---

[13] Franz E. Weinert and Rainer H. Kluwe, *Metacognition, Motivation, and Understanding* (Hillsdale, New Jersey: Lawrence Erlbaum Associates, 1987), 66. See Arthur L. Costa, ed., *Developing Minds: A Resource Book for Teaching Thinking* (Alexandria, VA: Association for Supervision and Curriculum Development, 1985), 307–337. The Appendices of this book are extremely helpful, particularly John Barell's "Self-Reflection on your Teaching: A Checklist" and Arthur L. Costa's "How Thoughtful Are Your Classrooms?"

[14] Jerome G. Kurfiss, *Critical Thinking: Theory, Research, Practice, Possibilities, ASHE-ERIC Higher Education Report No. 2* (Washington, D.C.: Association of the Study of Higher Education, 1988), 7.

[15] Ruth M. Loring, "Metacognitive Implementation of Journaling: A Strategy to Promote Reflective Teaching," in *Critical Thinking*, ed. Wendy Oxman and others, 256.

[16] Schubert M. Ogden, "Some Thoughts on a Christian Theology of Interreligious Dialogue," *Criterion* 33 no. 1 (Winter 1994): 5.

Dispositions of thoughtfulness also include a curiosity about new questions. Feminist theologians have uncovered subtle forms of sexism in canon law and in scripture itself. What will the churches do with this knowledge? Will they use it to put an end to discrimination, or will they try to ignore the questions raised by these theologians? Thoughtfulness also involves the flexibility to entertain alternative and original solutions to problems. For example, scientists at NASA believe that some form of life existed on Mars. Some theologians will argue that life cannot exist on other planets because that might put into doubt God's plan to save all of humanity. Others may find such an argument unconvincing asserting that Christ did save all of humanity and that those living on other planets need not be human. Thoughtfulness is crucial in generating the will to think and in developing those qualities of judgment that lead knowledge and skills in productive directions.[17]

Ill-structured Problems

Certain conditions are conducive to cultivating a literacy of thoughtfulness. One of these conditions is exposure to different viewpoints in the form of ill-structured problems. In religious studies, for example, one often meets ill-structured problems: Does God know that God is God? Are there any criteria for asserting that monotheism is superior to satanic worship? Is abortion ever justifiable for a Roman Catholic?

It seems to me that students have very little incentive to examine ideas reflectively without the experience of dealing with controversial issues. Why, for instance, do Christians claim that the Bible is the word of God yet doubt whether God inspired Mohammed the prophet to write the Qur'an? Professors of religion need to expose students to modes of reflective thinking more complex than the ones they currently employ.

To help students push their boundaries, utilize a series of open-ended questions: What are the various points of view on a particular issue, e.g., religious pluralism, contraception, etc.? How do the viewpoints differ? What assumptions do they have in common? What are the proposed solutions? Which one makes the most sense and why? What makes one viewpoint more compelling than another? Then challenge students to defend a position other than their own. Ask them to try to put themselves in the mind-set of their opponent. Some students may find this easier to do than others.[18]

---

17 Fred M. Newmann, "The Prospectus for Classroom Thoughtfulness in High School Social Studies," in *Teaching Thinking: An Agenda for the Twenty-First Century*, eds. Cathy Collins and John N. Mangieri (Hillsdale, New Jersey: Lawrence Erlbaum Associates, 1992), 107.

18 Carney Strange, "Beyond the Classroom: Encouraging Reflective Thinking," *Liberal Education* 78 No. 1 (Jan.–Feb. 1992): p. 30.

Encouraging Classroom Thoughtfulness

Several principles apply to thoughtfulness in the classroom, and several strategies encourage it. Concentrate on sustained examination of a few topics rather than the superficial coverage of many. In a course on theological ethics, for example, examine in depth certain topics such as genetic engineering, euthanasia, and contraception rather than trying to cover the entire range of issues dealing with bioethics. In course outlines, tell students explicitly that one of the course objectives will be to raise the level of thoughtfulness in the class. During the first week of the course, devote a class to the basics of critical thinking, paying special attention to metacognition. Keep in mind one question: How can I help my students become experts in my field of inquiry?

Learning may be defined as the process whereby novices become expert. Professors need to link new information to prior knowledge. How is this to be done? By using advance organizers and other bridging strategies such as metaphor. Faculty may simply tell students at the start of new material, "So far, we have looked at various definitions of religion. Now we will examine the writings of a very influential scholar in the history of religions, Mircea Eliade. Try to figure out for yourselves what his understanding of religion is based on reading the first chapter of his book."

Lessons need to contain substantive coherence and continuity. Jerome Bruner calls this learning the structure of a subject.[19] To learn structure means to learn how things are related. Teaching religious studies to undergraduates means to represent the structure of that subject in terms students can understand. To do this demands a thorough knowledge of the subject. The better a professor knows the subject, the better it can be taught.[20]

A key question I ask myself in teaching a lesson is this: How does a treatment of this subject relate to the course as a whole and to what we have previously studied? Not all courses are of equal difficulty in terms of deciding how they should be structured. An Introduction to Religion course has a very high degree of difficulty in terms of deciding what to cover and in what order and what to omit. A History of Christianity class, on the other hand, can utilize a chronological order, which is fairly easy to comprehend.

Students must be given sufficient time to think during the course; that is, they need time to prepare responses to questions. Some students will

---

[19] Jerome S. Bruner, *The Process of Education* (Cambridge: Harvard University Press, 1961), 7.

[20] Ibid., 40.

have a certain amount of resistance to those classes in which they are made to think. At the same time students must be given time to explore with each other and with themselves key questions that surface during the class. If I ask students a question and they cannot respond to it at the time, I tell them to think about it a minute, and then I get back to them after soliciting responses from other students. Tag important assertions with the student's name, the Julia Burch theory, for example, or the Sam Hayes response. In this way students see that their contributions are important to the class. Students then have an incentive for contributing even more to the discussion, confident that their comments will be taken seriously. This strategy also breaks down the "learning is storage" mentality that quietly asserts that professors are the experts and students are the clients. By breaking down this mentality, one sets the stage for the metaphor of learning wherein the teacher or professor is the midwife in the teaching-learning process and the real work is carried on by the students themselves.[21]

Another strategy to increase classroom thoughtfulness is to write a guiding question that defines the dominant problem on a handout. Tell students in class to try to come up with some tentative answers to the problem that you have posed. For example, I give students John Wisdom's parable of the gardener and ask them if the parable is on target in terms of the relationship between God and the world.

Ask challenging questions and structure challenging tasks. It is not difficult to ask profound questions. The trick is to find questions that can be answered and that take the student somewhere. This is where the art of teaching comes in. The teacher must construct a bridge to the difficult questions by laying the foundation of comprehendible and approachable questions.

An old adage states *virtus in medio stat*. This adage may be applied to the classroom situation. If one asks extremely difficult questions, few students will volunteer any answers. If the questions are too facile, the thoughtful students will lose interest. Instead, ask questions of moderate difficulty.

The Saturation Research Paper
I have used "saturation research" as an alternative approach to the term paper. In the traditional term paper students often merely restate the results of someone else's analysis, one in which they may have not a

---

[21] William J. Wooley, "Preparation for Leadership: Student-Oriented Teaching in Liberal Arts Colleges," in *A View From the Academy: Liberal Arts Professors on Excellent Teaching*, ed. Thomas Warren (Lanham: University Press of America, 1992), 152.

personal stake. It is more meaningful, and ultimately more useful, for students to select topics in which they have a personal investment.[22]

In the saturation research paper students interact with the information they are compiling and experience the excitement of grappling with the information in order to make their own connections. I give students "think time" in order to allow a topic of genuine interest to emerge for students. I ask students to saturate themselves in a historical figure and bring to life a significant event in that person's life, either by becoming that person or by becoming a witness to the event. I ask students to weave factual information together with such fictional techniques as interior monologue, dialogue, and description in order to create a "you are there" feeling in the reader.

Students are given directions such as 1) capture the event in present tense, as if it were happening now, 2) document sources with parenthetical references and a list of works cited, 3) adopt a viewpoint that is consistent throughout the narrative, and 4) use the conventions of written English effectively (grammar, sentence structure, spelling, etc.).

Before students begin their research, I have them read and discuss several student models, so that they can see first-hand how a range of papers are structured and to see the literary strategies previous writers have employed to bring the event to life. The saturation research paper increases student thoughtfulness because it makes students solve the problem of dramatizing history.[23]

Before the actual writing of the saturation paper, I take students through a series of brief exercises. I ask them to think about a significant event in their lives and to free write about it. This exercise allows students to make a connection between their lives and the life of their chosen character. To provide practice in decentering I ask students to put aside their free writes and to tell a partner their significant event. The partners, in turn, must re-create in writing the event they have just heard.

In order to get off to a good start, I tell students to write an opening page, which is read silently in class and commented upon by four other students. This reading allows writers to see the strategies four of their peers have used to set the stage for their historical incident. I find that students benefit more from receiving feedback during the writing process than after they have turned in their final products.

Writing the saturation research paper increases student thoughtfulness because it is essentially an interpretive encounter. Students must

---

[22] Carol Booth Olson, "Saturation Research: An Alternative Approach to the Research Paper," in *The Critical Writing Workshop: Designing Writing Assignments to Foster Critical Thinking*, ed. Toni-Lee Capossela (Portsmouth, New Hampshire: Boynton/Cook, 1993), 179.
[23] Ibid., 184.

use primary and secondary sources and then look within themselves to see history anew, thus making their own meaning. In the process students make a personal connection with the subject of their research. After students submit a first draft of their paper, it is scored by three students using the following guidelines:[24]

Figure 1.   Saturation Research Paper

The first draft of your paper received

Author _____   Score of _____

	Outstanding	Good	Needs Improvement
You displayed insight into the person and the significant event.			
As readers, we felt like we were there.			
You wove facts into your narrative very nicely.			
Your paper uses different fictional/ cinematic techniques.			
You use detailed writing to dramatize your character's moments and to convey your judgments and opinions.			
You use ample citations from your sources.			
You have few errors in the conventions of written English.			
What we liked best about your paper was . . .			
You might want to consider the following suggestions when you revise . . .			

[24] Ibid., 188.

Encourage classroom thoughtfulness by modeling thoughtfulness.[25] Instead of having a ready-made answer for every question, try to pause a few seconds, re-think a question, and answer it in a new and creative way. Start by telling students how your mind has changed on an issue. When asked why such tragedies as the death of a child, the fighting in Bosnia, or the lack of food in Rwanda happened, I often answered that it was God's will. Now I say to students that not all questions have answers. We don't know the answer to the mystery of evil. I feel more comfortable with this non-answer than with the cheap answers I once glibly gave.

Summary

One may distinguish between three levels of learning: declarative knowledge, strategic knowledge, and metacognition. Many professors overemphasize lower-order thinking and are so worried about covering the material that they overlook strategic knowledge on the skills level. They also fail to cultivate a literacy of thoughtfulness.

Strategic or procedural knowledge describes what a person can do: manage time, organize information, and "deep process" information. All of these are skills understood as the ability to use the knowledge one possesses.

In the first part of this chapter we discussed five skills that are related to "getting ready to learn," namely, 1) self-evaluation, which is one's ability to assess learning skills that we may (or may not) possess; 2) goal setting: setting a direction and then developing a plan to get there; 3) time management: scheduling, evaluating time use, and exploring changes in time management; 4) monitoring attitudes: both consciously controlling one's attention level and "power thinking"; and 5) motivation that wells up from within the learner as he or she gains satisfaction from achieving a goal (intrinsic) or receives some reward, incentive, or goal extrinsic to the task (extrinsic motivation).

The second section addresses learning skills and answers the question of how one acquires, retrieves, and retains these skills. Five key skills are involved in answering this question. They are 1) locating information in religious studies, 2) selecting information, 3) organizing information, 4) communicating information, and 5) training memory, which assumes that there are specific skills that can increase the mind's ability to remember, retain, and retrieve information. One may, for instance, use "deep processing" to consciously generate emotions and linguistic information about a thought, image, or sensation.

---

25 Newmann, 114.

The third level of learning may be termed *metacognition,* or a literacy of thoughtfulness. Metacognition involves knowledge of, and control of, one's own cognitive system. It includes such control strategies as asking questions, taking notes, setting goals, making plans, observing the effectiveness of one's work, and making corrective changes. This section suggested various strategies to help students become more thoughtful learners and discussed several ways to encourage classroom thoughtfulness, such as sustained examination of a few topics in a course as opposed to the superficial coverage of many; asking challenging questions and structuring challenging tasks; and modeling thoughtfulness on the part of the professor. This final suggestion is based on the adage "Don't tell me what to do; show me."

Part of critical thinking includes the active involvement of students in their own education in accordance with the adage "It is better to do one's education rather than to receive it." The next chapter contains a careful analysis of "active learning." It occurs when faculty do more than simply talk to students.

4

Teaching in the Active Mode

*"One must learn by doing the thing, for though you think you
know it—you have no certainty, until you try."*

Sophocles

Most students will neither develop their thinking skills nor engage
themselves in the content of a course unless they are forced to become
active learners.[1] Active learning is part of critical thinking because active
learning makes students responsible for their own learning and encourages them to think for themselves. Active learning may be described in
various ways. In this chapter active learning refers to instructional strategies that involve students in doing things and reflecting about what they
are doing.[2]

This chapter consists of three sections. Part I speaks of active learning
in general, followed in Part II by a discussion of some theoretical issues
involved in active learning. Part III looks at additional strategies promoting active learning, such as in-class writing, problem solving, and peer
teaching.

I. What Is Active Learning?

Active learning occurs when students *do* something besides listening to
the teacher. It may be distinguished from passive learning, which takes
place when students are merely receptacles of knowledge as they listen

[1] Stanley J. Michalak, "Enhancing Critical-Thinking Skills in Traditional Liberal Arts
Courses: Report on a Faculty Workshop," *Liberal Education* 72 (Fall 1986): 256. See Chet Meyers and Thomas B. Jones, *Promoting Active Learning: Strategies for the College Classroom* (San
Francisco: Jossey-Bass Publishers, 1993) especially pp. 3–56. Teachers in an active-learning
classroom direct/choreograph what happens so that students take responsibility for their
own learning.

[2] Charles C. Bonwell and James A. Eison, *Active Learning: Creating Excitement in the Classroom, ASHE-ERIC Higher Education Report No. 1* (Washington, D.C.: The George Washington
University, 1991) iii. See Richard Penaskovic and John von Eschenbach, "Infusing Critical Thinking into the Academic Study of Religion," *Spotlight on Teaching* Vol. 7, No. 4 (November, 1992) 8–10. For a more extensive treatment, see John C. Bean, *Engaging Ideas: The
Professor's Guide to Integrating Writing, Critical Thinking, and Active Learning in the Classroom*
(San Francisco: Jossey-Bass Publishers, 1996).

to lectures and record the important points. The lecture method focuses on recall. However, lectures often fail to provide students with opportunities to search for insights on their own or to perceive meaning.[3]

Active learning and the lecture method are not antithetical; it is not a question of using one method or the other. The methods complement each other. For example, some faculty who lecture primarily incorporate many techniques of active learning into their lectures. To praise the merits of active learning does not mean to denigrate the benefits of the lecture. The lecture method is invaluable when the instruction needs to cover large amounts of material. However, lecturers should be able to make their instruction more effective by paying attention to the concerns raised in this chapter.[4]

Active learning puts a premium on developing students' intellectual skills, particularly for higher-order thinking tasks such as analysis, synthesis, evaluation, and critical judgment. Active learning requires teachers to be leaders as they invent work at which students experience success so that classrooms become truly student-centered. In a course on scripture, for instance, I may ask students to share that chapter of the Hebrew Scriptures that speaks to them most in terms of their own lives. Students are then divided into small groups to discuss the reasons they chose a particular chapter. By engaging in such an exercise, students are made to come to terms with the biblical texts themselves.

Active Learning as a Process
Active learning is a process that has the following characteristics:

1) Active learning assumes that students have a positive contribution to make to the learning process based on their knowledge, experience, and abilities. Learning is a two-way street. Much of what I know about the academic study of religion I have learned from my students. The students' questions keep me alert, forcing me to be *au courant* both in my material and in my pedagogy. My students are fascinated by New Age religion and wanted me to discuss it in an Introduction to Religion course. I had to bone up on the subject myself before I could tell students about it.

2) Active learning maintains that the primary responsibility for learning should be shared with students. I do this in several ways. First, I use cooperative learning groups and have students select other students as group leaders who are responsible for making sure that the work of the group is accomplished. Second, I make students responsible for read-

3 Stanley J. Michalak, 255.

4 Robert W. Cole and Philip C. Schlechly, "Teachers as Trailblazers," *Educational Horizons* 70 No. 3 (Spring 1992): 136.

ing the assigned books by testing them on some of the readings not explicitly covered in the class. Third, although I do not require class attendance, I have four unannounced five-point quizzes during the term. Often these quizzes demand a knowledge of the assigned readings. My examinations are a forceful reminder that students are responsible for their own learning.

3) Active learning makes the teacher a catalyst for learning. I try to see what students' needs are and to help them attain their learning goals. I have students explicitly reflect on this question: How do you learn best? I usually ask them to take out a piece of paper and write a short essay on their answer, and then we talk about this. I receive much valuable information from students and am surprised at the multiple ways that they learn. For example, my classes are discussion-centered. I often ask one student to summarize the comments of another student. They never know when they will be called upon to sum up another student's comments, and hence they learn by really listening to their peers.

4) Active learning starts with the desires, needs, and perceptions of students. Instructors have to constantly ask themselves this question: How can I make this particular class student-centered? What are the students' needs today?

5) To teach actively means to structure the learning process so that it supports students in both clarifying and expressing their needs. How does one know students' needs? The instructor should ask them. If students come to my office to ask a question about the course, I ask them how they are doing in the course. Is it meeting their needs? This informal feedback helps me understand the needs of my students, and these needs change from class to class, semester to semester.

6) Active learning also assumes that the most useful assessment for students is self-assessment; that is why four weeks into a particular course I ask students to take out a piece of paper and answer these kinds of questions: How are you doing in this course? Comment on the readings and your degree of involvement in the course. If you were teaching this course, would you do anything differently? How could this course be structured better to increase your learning? What do you like about the class? Should there be more discussion, more tests, more audiovisuals? Have the wheels within your own head started clicking? Do you see where this course is going? I take these student comments and divide them into three categories: positive, negative, and suggestions for improvement. I have my work-study student type and run them off so I can give students feedback on how their peers feel about the class. Most of the suggestions are easy to implement. For example, some students may have trouble hearing me speak while others may have difficulty seeing the blackboard.

7) Active learning is a process that empowers students to actively engage themselves in learning. I try to get students "turned on" to the subject matter. For instance, in teaching a History of Christianity course, I try to excite students about church history so that they want to read more than is expected.

I try to make explicit connections between the course content and some hot issues today. For example, in discussing the Reformation in the sixteenth century I ask whether Martin Luther's dictum that *Ecclesia semper reformanda* holds true today, are the churches constantly in need of renewal and reform?

I tell students pertinent anecdotes about the historical figures under consideration that are not found in the standard textbooks. For example, when I was a graduate student in Munich in the 1960s I went to a dance and met a girl named Anna Barth. I asked her if she had ever heard of a great theologian by the name of Karl Barth, and to my astonishment she said that Karl Barth was her grandfather. If students get into a glow about the study of religion, they learn more.[5]

II. Issues of Active Learning

Every training event has both a text and a subtext. The text comprises the content of the training experience and the strategies used to communicate that content to the learner. The subtext, on the other hand, involves the relationship of the trainer to learners as individuals and as a group. The subtext is the emotional climate found in any particular classroom as a result of the interaction between professor and students. And as Baldwin and Williams point out, to construct an active learning scenario that works, teachers must understand the intrinsic reluctance of the student to learn in unfamiliar ways.[6]

Power and Authority

The first issue is that of power and authority. Power is found in the person or in the situation. In any classroom the teacher has power over the

---

[5] Roger H. Garrison, "The Tools of the Teaching Trade," *Improving College and University Teaching* 23–24 (1975–76): 70. For an excellent discussion of critical thinking, cooperative learning, and electronic learning, see Dennis Adams and Mary Hamm, *New Designs for Teaching and Learning: Promoting Active Learning in Tomorrow's Schools* (San Francisco: Jossey-Bass Publishers, 1994), 15–112. See Patricia A. Backer and Joseph K. Yabu, "Hypermedia as an Instructional Resource," in *Changing College Classrooms: New Teaching and Learning Strategies for an Increasingly Complex World* eds. Diane F. Halpern and Associates, (San Francisco: Jossey-Bass Publishers, 1994), 230–253.

[6] Jill Baldwin and Hank Williams, *Active Learning: A Trainer's Guide* (Oxford: Blackwell Education, 1988), 7.

students. Authority, on the other hand, is given to the teacher by others—in this case, students. In active learning the focus of power shifts from the professor to the students. In the traditional classroom situation learners have very little power. They are told both what to learn and how to learn it, often with little regard to whether it is of any use to them or attention to how best it could be presented to them. The professor needs to be powerful in order to share power in a learning situation. Power is what a professor starts with in teaching a class, but how he or she uses that power determines whether the students grant him or her authority.

Students look for several characteristics in an instructor: knowledge of the subject matter, fairness, competence as a teacher, and the like. Students also want a teacher to have energy and to energize them. They also expect an intuitive sympathy with the group that will provide incentive to give the teacher authority. It amazes me how much students will insist on seeing the instructor as powerful, however much the instructor tries to share power with them in the classroom. Perhaps students do not want to feel powerful in the classroom because power demands they take responsibility for their own learning. For these reasons some students have an investment in the instructor's holding onto the power, and this investment can clash with the instructor's investment in making students take more control. What we need then is a balance of power. We need as professors to give students the power they need, yet at the same time to retain enough power to carry on.[7]

Students unaccustomed to having power may resist the professor's desire to share power. What can a particular instructor do if he or she encounters such resistance? One way to handle this is for the instructor to reveal his or her own vulnerabilities. A simple way to reveal one's vulnerabilities is to tell students one does not know the answer to a particular question. In student-centered or active learning, instructors draw more on their own personalities than on their positions in order to have power in the learning situation. For example, I use humor at times and students respond very well to it. I once told a student he did not have to come up for his grade: I would roll it down to him.

The Classroom Climate

Climate is an important ingredient in all learning, both active and passive. In order for active learning to work, one must create a climate that will allow students to move beyond what they have expected. At the beginning of a course students are more interested in what they are going to learn rather than in how they are going to learn. By involving them immediately in clarifying the content of the course, we begin to involve

7 Jill Baldwin and Hank Williams, 32.

them in the process, or the *how*, of the course, and as the course progresses the *why* and the *how* become increasingly interconnected.[8]

The first step in managing the climate is to analyze the existing climate in the particular classroom situation. Where and how students sit at the beginning of the course are indicators of the level of anxiety that they are feeling. Some students will feel excluded if there are small groups of individuals who know each other. I believe that it is important on the first day of class to get to the classroom early to mingle with the students before the actual class begins, to talk to them informally as they enter the classroom, and to create a positive atmosphere in which they feel welcome. In reading the existing climate, begin with this question: What level of openness and trust exists in the classroom at the beginning of the course? Assess the foundation on which you must build.

A welcoming atmosphere tells students a little bit about you and what you expect the course to be. In other words, how the introduction is made has considerable impact on the climate. The instructor models caring, open, dynamic behavior for the class to follow. One can also project a high energy level.[9]

It is important that students know what is expected of them. This means we must make our course objectives explicit. To teach active learning, this has to be spelled out in the course syllabus. By knowing what is expected of them, students begin thinking about what they will have to do to succeed. Some may decide to drop the course.

Providing reassurance also lets students know that they can make mistakes in the course without being ridiculed. This is part and parcel of creating a safe environment where students know they will not be put down by other students or the instructor. A useful strategy I use in my classes is the "smile and pass" rule: if I call on a student by name, John Doe, and John does not know the answer, he can smile and pass. I will go on to someone else and ask the question again. The "smile and pass" rule has two important benefits: 1) it prevents embarrassment. No one wants to feel stupid if he or she does not know the answer to a particular question. 2) It allows an instructor to ask questions and to call students back into the class who are daydreaming or distracted. It is up to the instructor to maintain a balance between comfort and security and a readiness to face challenges and to take personal risks.

Make students active in the classroom. I do this by having students leave their seats on the first or second day of class to get acquainted with one another and then reflecting on that experience. This exercise releases the energy in the classroom by having students meet other students

---

8 Ibid., 70 ff.
9 Ibid., 72.

and form small groups to discuss the topic assigned for the day. I use a get-acquainted exercise that I call "The Cocktail Party." Students write four adjectives to describe themselves on one side of an index card. On the other side, they write general information: name, address, phone number, and major. They tape the card to their lapel, with the option of displaying either side. At a given signal I ask the students to rise and mingle. Their objective is to get acquainted with every student in class. They can read each classmate's card, and they have the option of asking each student to turn over the card so they can read the other side. However, the student has the option of declining to turn over the other side of the card. This works in classes that range from forty to 100 students.

If a student is able to put down the four adjectives to describe himself or herself and to meet and mingle with other students, it shows a certain amount of openness. In my experience students who are content with showing their name and impersonal information about themselves are probably going to be more anxious about the class and not as open as students who are willing to share their four adjectives.

Another version of this exercise involves having students pick a partner for a paired discussion. For instance, partners can talk about their hopes and fears for the course. Then these pairs can move into groups of four. Once students feel comfortable discussing things in small units, they are much more likely to want to discuss them in larger groups.[10]

A welcoming climate must be created at the start of the course, but it must also be nurtured throughout the course for learning to take place effectively. Instructors with large classes of 100 or more are faced with integrating students signing up late for a course. As many as fifteen to twenty students may have missed the basic introduction and orientation and thus do not know what climate has already been established. Instructors need to at least summarize some of the main points they have made in the introduction, and they must pay attention to the dynamics in the classroom with the addition of these students. All the students in the classroom should feel free to express their feelings and be receptive to the expression of the feelings of others. Again, it is the instructor's job to pay attention to this dimension, to make the students in the classroom aware of the climate, and to encourage the class to take some responsibility for the classroom climate.

Support
Support is an ingredient in the climate, but it may also be considered an element in itself. The aim is to create a learning environment in which students support each other in three ways: 1) by sharing responses, 2) by

10 Ibid., 78.

encouraging involvement in the course, and 3) by enabling students to take action. To help students, the instructor must hear the feelings that lie behind questions that students ask.[11] For example, students in my History of Christianity course recently asked this question: Do I have to read chapters five through eight of the textbook? It was not clear to me, at first, why they were asking this question, but in the course of our discussion it became clear that students were feeling overburdened. They were concerned about the amount of reading required for this ten-week course, namely, three required textbooks and book reports on two other books. Students' concerns are not always expressed openly. Sometimes I have to ask myself what students are really getting at in their questions.

Why is support necessary in a classroom? Primarily because learning involves change, and change is often resisted. Students are reassured by sharing their feelings of doubt and anxiety with others. When learners feel supported, they are prepared to meet new challenges. Challenge occurs whenever the existing framework of the learner is disturbed. It is particularly important that students support each other in active learning as the role of the teacher becomes secondary. In student-centered learning the relationship among the learners is more important than the relationship between the learners and the teacher.

The teacher must build rapport within the classroom that will enable students to help one another learn. In a large class, the instructor may divide the students into smaller groups so that support can develop. I think it is important to form different groups for different activities so that all class members have contact with other students in the class. Instead of allowing students to form their own groups for discussion, in a class of twenty-five I assign everyone a number from one to five. Then five groups form randomly. Hence all students will come in contact with other students in the classroom if that system is used throughout the term.I also use snowballing to help students become supportive of each other in the classroom. We form groups of two to discuss a particular question. These students team up with another pair to form a group of four to discuss the question. These combine to form a group of eight, then maybe a group of sixteen. This helps support groups to arise within the classroom.[12]

11 Ibid., 87. See Robert G. Kraft, "Group Inquiry Turns Passive Students Active," *College Teaching* 33 no. 4 (1985): 149–154.

12 Ibid., 82. For some ideas on teaching in a student-centered classroom, see Elizabeth Aaronsohn, *Going Against the Grain: Supporting the Student-Centered Teacher* (Thousand Oaks, CA: Corwin Press, Inc., 1996), 53–73. Although written for elementary and secondary school teachers, some of these ideas may be adopted by college professors.

Another concept in active learning is called stepping. Stepping involves structuring the class in such a way that students experience learning as a series of developments. It affects both the shape and the depth of the class: the shape by giving a sense of movement from a starting point to a conclusion and the depth by giving a sense of movement from the superficial to the profound. If, for example, a class is presented with activities that are too difficult, the students are likely to feel inadequate or threatened or to throw up their hands and say "We can't do this." It also helps gain the commitment of students to the idea that content and process are of equal importance in terms of their own development, both professional and personal.[13]

Setting Up Challenges
Another concept I call challenge. Challenge is integral to development, and both are concerned primarily with movement. I find that in active learning students face more risks than in passive learning. Doing is always riskier than learning passively because doing involves testing understanding, applying understanding, being exposed to others, and risking failure. In active learning students must expose their personalities and knowledge to the critical responses of their peers. They are also challenged to apply their learning in a rigorous testing of understanding, which exposes any laziness. It also may challenge the students' assumptions.[14]

In an Introduction to Religious Studies course, for instance, a handful of students always assume that Christianity is vastly superior to other world religions. I challenge these students by asking them how much they really know about other religions. Have they read the Qur'an or the Buddhist Scriptures? Is it possible to understand another religion from the outside? Does a believer in another religion see some things differently than an outsider? Thus challenged in their opinions, students must rethink their assumptions.

Application
Application makes students see the implications of their learning and challenges them to review their pre-course experience in the light of that learning. To apply new learning requires students to be creative and imaginative with what they have learned. The instructor has to walk a tightrope in terms of challenge. One does not want to challenge students

---

[13] Ibid., 87. See Lawrence P. Litecky, "Great Teaching, Great Learning: Classroom Climate, Innovative Methods, and Critical Thinking," *New Directions for Community Colleges* 77 (Spring 1992): 83–90.
[14] Ibid., 95.

too much or too little. For example, a guest speaker in my Introduction to Religion class was an agnostic. He called into question many of the students' sacred beliefs. In processing his talk during the following class, I pointed out some logical inconsistencies in his position. In doing so I showed students how one must be critical of another viewpoint while acknowledging its positive features.

As an instructor, I monitor small-group discussion. The teacher's primary role is to make sure that enough time is available for groups to think through what they are learning and to evaluate the experience. It does not make sense to assume that students got the point of a particular exercise. The point has to be made explicit, and the teacher has to set aside class time for reflection.[15]

Reflecting students process information, give information meaning, and learn from it in special ways. In active learning, reflection must be structured into the course. As Williams and Baldwin point out, students rarely structure their reflection appropriately to the nature of the experience.[16] But without structured reflection, the transfer of learning from the course to real life will be minimal and will be vulnerable to learning decay. Students rarely come to a course with clear expectations or with the sense of how this particular course fits in with the rest of their lives. For this reason it makes sense to tell students at the outset of the course what they are supposed to learn from it and how this course fits in with other courses in religion. Later, on reflection, they are able to test their findings against the original purpose of the course.

In order to give this reflection structure, ask students in pairs to think about their assignment and to share with one another what they have learned from a particular exercise. Have a group reflect on the learning its members have made during an exercise, using a variety of teaching methods such as 1) a group summary on a flip chart, 2) a taped group discussion, 3) a symbolic drawing or chart of what they have learned, 4) a group presentation, or 5) a written interpretation of what others have said. By having structured reflection, students can then connect what they have learned to their own lives. This is a process of integration. This, too, may be structured by asking students to identify specific steps they can take on their return to work or the dormitory to make meaningful what they learned in a particular class.

Structured reflection requires students to be calm (so that they can be attuned to what is occurring within their psyche), thoughtful, and sensitive. In setting up structured reflection, it makes sense to use a variety of approaches, such as students reflecting on their own about what they

15 Ibid., 106.
16 Ibid., 108.

got out of a course; students reflecting in pairs, small groups, or large groups; and using writing, talking, drawing, and demonstrations. In all of this the teacher is the facilitator or catalyst.[17]

One of the teacher's main jobs will be to get students to personalize their responses instead of generalizing them. In any learning situation one cannot totally plan for students' reactions. Students bring to the course a whole set of feelings toward themselves, toward others, toward the course, and toward the instructor. For this reason teachers must pay attention to the resistance of students toward learning. Resistance has to be dealt with openly; otherwise, it can sabotage the teaching efforts of even the best instructors.[18]

Resistance: A Natural Response to a Challenge
Resistance may be called a strategy by which students avoid taking risks in class. Resistance is a natural response to challenge. If students are valued in a class, they will be less afraid of taking risks. Students with low self-esteem are often more concerned about preserving their self-images than about taking risks. Sometimes a class needs to experience some turbulence in order to move to a new level of insight or openness. I find it necessary to confront a student or students at times on a particular issue. In confronting students, I point out their resistance explicitly and deal with it.[19] I do not confront students publicly. For instance, if a student misses several days of classes without an explanation, I ask to see that student privately to learn what exactly is going on. Whatever the student's response, we can clear the air and I can then give the student extra help.

III. Practical Implementation

This section discusses how active learning can be applied to the academic study of religion, concentrating on several techniques that I have found useful. Active learning can be used in conjunction with the lecture. Many variations are possible. There is, first of all, the guided lecture, where students are made to listen to a twenty- to thirty-minute talk without taking any notes.[20] Then they are told to take five minutes and write what they remember, spending the rest of the time in small groups clarifying the material. Students are surprised when this format is first proposed. It helps the instructor get an idea of what students see as

17 Ibid., 109.
18 Ibid., 112.
19 Ibid., 126.
20 Ibid., 158.

important in the material, but it also allows students to get information from their peers that they missed in the lecture itself.

The Modified Lecture
Research suggests that the exclusive use of lecture in the classroom constrains students' learning.[21] In the modified lecture strategy the instructor pauses two to three minutes three times during the lecture. During the pauses, students have a chance to work in pairs to discuss and rework their notes. They also have the opportunity to ask their partners what they have missed. This is a minor strategy, but it is highly effective.

About one-third of the students in my eleven o'clock classes say that they have listened to lectures for three straight hours before my class. It takes a lot of energy to listen to someone speak for a long time. Psychologists point out that about 50 percent of what the professor says is never heard by students for various reasons: daydreaming, inattention, or inability to listen because it takes so much energy. It makes sense to use strategic pauses in lectures.[22]

It also makes sense for students to take an exam right after a lecture. Scheduling an exam or quiz stimulates students to study. Hence, short quizzes and tests are a method of active learning. Another device that can be used effectively to break up the class lecture, particularly if one teaches on the quarter system in which classes typically meet five days a week, is to set aside one day a week for open-ended, student-generated questions on any aspect of the course. If it is a small class of thirty-five students or fewer, we sit in a circle and play "Twenty Questions."

The Game of Twenty Questions
The idea is to ask me questions dealing with the course material or any part of the course.[23] The more experienced the teacher and the more familiar the teacher is with the material at hand, the more comfortable the teacher will be with this technique. But it really is not that difficult. One does not have to know everything as a teacher. Ask students to look something up. Say, "I'm not sure, but I'll get back to the class tomorrow on this topic." It helps to be humble.

Another way to get students to think while asking questions is to have students explain why their particular question is important. These student questions can also serve as topics for lectures the following days, particularly if a question is asked that has no simple answer or that will take a long time to answer.

[21] Charles C. Bonwell and James A. Eison, 12.
[22] Ibid., 8.
[23] Ibid., 10.

Large Classes: Is Active Learning Possible?
What about large classes? Are they necessarily a barrier to active learning? Research indicates that students engage in less analysis, synthesis, and evaluation in classes of more than sixteen students.[24] In one study 71 percent of the interactions in large classes were at the lowest level, namely, that of memorizing information.[25] However, students' negative attitudes toward large classes can be changed if the instructor does certain things: 1) clearly outlines the course objectives, 2) uses a variety of instructional strategies, 3) and makes use of visual media. I would argue that not class size *per se* but the method of instruction (if active learning is used) seems to be the major ingredient of learning.[26] Even a large class can be personalized. I teach about 100 students in World Religions and in Introduction to Religion, and I use several strategies to personalize the class. I arrive before class, talk to students, and move around during class. I personally return examinations and put comments on their exams and sign my name. I learn students' names and recognize them by name in class. I use humor, and I brainstorm a topic before lecturing: before a lecture on Hinduism, I will ask students what they associate with the word *India*. I also break the class up into small learning groups. All of these strategies can create the perception of a small working space.[27]

The Importance of Asking Questions
A goal of mine is to get students to ask and answer questions. It has been my experience that students are more likely to think when they are asked to write and speak, and that is the great value of questions, whether you have students ask questions in class or ask them to jot down their answers on a small piece of paper. Classroom questioning should take place in a supportive classroom environment, and the personalizing techniques mentioned can be used to help students feel comfortable about asking questions.

The students' most legitimate question goes like this: Of what use is this course to me?[28] This is a question I ask students to think about several times during the quarter or semester. It helps to create an emotional

24 Ibid., 14.

25 Ibid., 15.

26 Ibid., 15.

27 Ibid., 16. On managing a technology-rich classroom, see Judith Haymore Sandholtz, et al, *Teaching With Technology: Creating Student-Centered Classrooms* (New York and London: Teachers College Press, 1996), 55–75. For some ideas on personalizing a large lecture class, see Barbara Gross Davis, *Tools for Teaching* (San Francisco: Jossey-Bass Publishers, 1993), 125–139 and J. Geske, "Overcoming the Drawbacks of the Large Lecture Class," *College Teaching* Vol. 40, No. 4 (1992), 151–154.

28 Roger H. Garrison, 70.

climate that encourages students to take risks. The professor does this by projecting openness and predictability, by encouraging students to formulate their own views, and by learning students' names. I find it helpful not only to remember students' names but also to ask them at the start of the semester what name they want to be called. I once had a student whose real name was Timothy but who wanted to be called Elmo. By calling him Elmo, I was able to establish rapport with him. People have very strong feelings about their names, and the more you can call them the names with which they feel comfortable, the more they feel part of the class.

Types of Questions
It is helpful to remember that a teacher may ask various types of questions. Most questions are memory questions. Only 18 percent of classroom questions require higher-order thinking skills. Studies show that about one-third of the questions asked in the classroom receive no response from students.[29] There are open-ended questions, such as "What role will religion play in world affairs in the '90s?" There are also evaluative questions. For example, what are the strengths and weaknesses of the textbook chosen for the Introduction to the New Testament course? In thinking about the types of questions, it helps to pay attention to Bloom's *Taxonomy*.

In Bloom's *Taxonomy* the lowest level of questions concern knowledge. They answer the questions who, what, when, where, and how. Second-level questions deal with comprehension. "Retell the story we have just discussed in class" is a comprehension question.[30]

Application questions require the use of facts, rules, and principles. For example, why is the study of symbol significant in the academic study of religion? How is the David Koresh tragedy at Waco, Texas, related to the Jim Jones mass suicide? Or where do you find an example of parallelism in the Psalms?

A fourth type of question deals with analysis, or the separation of a whole into its component parts. An example would be "What are the classic divisions of theology?" Or "How does Alexandrian theology compare and contrast with Antiochene theology?" Another analytical question would ask for evidence on the two-source theory in New Testament studies or for the features of the academic study of religion that distinguish it from theology.

A fifth level of questioning employs synthesis to combine ideas to form a new whole. An example of a synthetic query would be this: What

[29] Bonwell and Eison, 24.
[30] Benjamin S. Bloom and others, eds., *Taxonomy of Educational Objectives: The Classification of Educational Goals* (New York: David McKay Company, Inc.), 89.

would you infer from the fact that the Muslim religion will have the most adherents by the year 2000? What effect will this have on world religions? What concrete steps would you suggest for bringing about a dialogue between Christians and Muslims? Another example: What might happen if you combined the Unification Church with the Church of Jesus Christ of the Latter Day Saints? Or how would one create or design a new world religion? What features would be essential to it?

The sixth type of question is evaluative.[31] Evaluation has to do with the development of opinions, judgments, or decisions. "What is the most important god in Hinduism and why?" is an example. Others would be: How would you decide about the morality of having an abortion? What criteria would you use to assess the credibility or trust-worthiness of the four Gospels? Can you place the following in order of priority: a) the Hadiths, b) the Sunnah, c) the Qu'ran, d) the Shariah?

Some Rules for Asking Questions

Vary the kinds of questions you ask, including some from all levels. Be clear and specific.[32] Rather than asking a broad question like "What did you learn from chapter one?" ask "What does an eschatological concept mean?" Clarity, in other words, increases the likelihood that students will respond effectively. Questions have to be adapted to the students' level of ability. What might be an appropriate question for a senior who majors in religion may be inappropriate for a freshman. It also helps to ask questions logically and sequentially and to follow up on students' responses to the questions that are given. Keep a deliberative silence after asking the questions. Asking many questions back to back will make students feel as though they are being interrogated. Invite students to elaborate or ask another student to build on the answer previously given. It is also helpful to report back what the students have said. This may also encourage others to raise questions about this issue.[33]

Many professors fail to give students enough time in responding to a question. I recommend keeping quiet three to five seconds after asking a question.

Visual-based Instruction

Surprisingly enough, research indicates that visual-based instruction is not significantly better than lecturing because watching a film does not actively involve students in a class anymore than listening to a lecture

---

31 Ibid., 185.
32 Bonwell and Eison, 28.
33 Ibid.

does. However, visual-based learning does have a significant impact as a source of feedback for acquiring skills such as typing, working on a computer, playing tennis, and the like. Videotapes are best used to stimulate class discussion or to spawn short essays that analyze the implications of the events shown.

Writing as a Way of Learning

Essay writing and other writing genre are important in active learning. The idea that writing is a way of learning more about every subject is one of the basic presuppositions in the writing-across-the-curriculum movement. Research shows that writing assignments improve students' writing skills and their learning of the subject. It does not matter whether the instructor evaluates the written assignments or not. It does not depend on the type of written assignments. They all seem to be effective in getting students to think. As a basic rule, the instructor should use a wide variety of writing tasks such as keeping a journal, when appropriate, or summarizing an assigned reading. Have students compose an essay prescribing a solution to a problem presented in class. Then the students can be broken up into pairs to grade each other's essays. The choice of writing assignment depends on the goal the instructor has in giving a particular assignment. If the goal is comprehension, then students might be asked to write an essay that summarizes the material. However, if the goal is to focus students' attention on concepts and relationships, an analytical essay would be best.[34]

A case study can serve well in promoting class discussion. A case study that is based on real-life incidents is especially good in eliciting student interest. Such a study also helps foster higher-order thinking because students have to apply their knowledge to a case in which there is no one right answer. Case studies are beneficial in helping students change their attitudes.[35]

Cooperative Learning

Another strategy to promote active learning is called cooperative learning. In cooperative learning, groups of four to six students work together. Then a worksheet of two to six questions is prepared for the days' discussion. Each student must submit a written answer to the worksheet as the requirement for participation in the group's discussion. I find it helpful to pass out the instruction sheet, which spells out responsibilities for students in a small-group discussion. Each group must write a report as a result of the discussion. This written report contains the major ideas

---

[34] Ibid., 37.
[35] Ibid., 39.

expressed in the discussion. It also contains points of agreement and disagreement in the group, and grades are given to the report developed in
class. Usually I assign a group grade. However, I occasionally assign a
grade to each student if a particular group requests it. Studies show that
cooperative learning has positive effects on students' self-esteem. It also
promotes good relations in the classroom, and it encourages students to
cooperate rather than compete and often spills over into other settings.[36]

There is also room for role-playing, simulation, and games. The difference between role-playing and games is this: games and simulations
can last several hours or several days, but role-playing usually involves
less time—an hour or less. The instructor's job is to structure the situation by providing background details and a general sketch of the roles
to be played. It is even possible for an instructor to debate himself or
herself by arguing both sides of an issue. On Monday I may argue in
favor of abortion, and the next day I may point out its down side.[37]

By using a variety of teaching methods, one is able to reach students
who have different learning styles. What if a particular instructor has not
used active learning and wants to implement it in his or her classroom?
Several things must be kept in mind. First, identify those strategies you
currently employ; then determine which new techniques will be suitable
to use on a trial basis next term. Some strategies promoting active learning are more easily implemented in some disciplines than in others.[38]

Summary

Active learning refers to instructional strategies that involve students in
doing something besides listening to the professor. This chapter looked
at several theoretical issues involved in active learning, such as the relationship between power and authority; classroom climate; and support,
challenge, and reflection.

How does active learning apply to the academic study of religion?
Various strategies such as the guided lecture, the modified lecture, the
use of questions, in-class writing, and cooperative learning can all be uti-
lized to make students active partners in their own education.

Closely related to the concept of active learning is cooperative or collaborative learning. This forms the subject of our next chapter.

[36] Ibid., 47.
[37] Ibid., 48.
[38] Ibid., 67.

5

Cooperative Learning

"No man can become rich without himself enriching others."
Andrew Carnegie

Cooperative learning refers to the instructional use of small groups so that students work together to increase their own and each other's learning. Its historical roots go back to John Dewey's work on experiential learning and the research of Kurt Lewin and Martin Deutsch on small-group theory. Educators know a great deal about the effectiveness of cooperative learning. Solid research has demonstrated the effectiveness of working in small groups as opposed to the traditional style of learning.

This chapter contains an extended discussion of the social skills students need in order to work successfully in small groups. Students must have a variety of skills such as listening, paraphrasing, and doing a perception check in order to profit from cooperative learning. Particular attention is given to the role of discussion in cooperative learning. This chapter concludes by noting some problem areas as faculty attempt to implement critical thinking into the religious studies curriculum.

Student-to-student interaction may be structured in three ways: (1) competitively, that is, as a competitive enterprise in which students work hard to outdo their peers or take it easy because they see little chance in doing so. Most lecture classes are structured this way; (2) individualistically, in which students focus on their own self-interest and ignore the success or failure of their peers. In this case, students work at their own pace, have their own goals, and realize that the achievement of their goals remains unrelated to what other students do; and (3) cooperatively, where students work together to achieve shared goals.[1]

---

[1] David W. Johnson, Roger T. Johnson and Karl A. Smith, *Cooperative Learning: Increasing College Faculty Instructional Productivity* (Washington, D.C.: George Washington University, 1991) 3. See Barbara Gross Davis, *Tools for Teaching* (San Francisco: Jossey-Bass Publishers, 1993) 147–158; Kris Bosworth and Sharon J. Hamilton. *Collaborative Learning: Underlying Processes and Effective Techniques* (San Francisco: Jossey-Bass Publishers, 1994); Robert E. Slavin, *Cooperative learning, Theory, Research and Practice*, Second Edition, (Boston: Allyn and Bacon, 1995); Tracey E. Sutherland and Charles C. Bonwell, eds., *Using Active Learning in*

What kind of mix should one have for a course in religious studies? I believe in using cooperative learning at least 60 percent of the time with the remainder given over to individualistic and competitive learning activities.

A Definition of Cooperative Learning

Cooperative learning may be defined as the instructional use of small groups so that students work together to increase their own and one another's learning. Some authors refer to cooperative learning as learning communities, collaborative learning, peer teaching, team learning, study circles, or collective learning.

Historical Roots

Cooperative learning has its historical basis in student-centered instruction and experiential learning theories associated with John Dewey, Jean Piaget, and L.S. Vygotsky. These educators stressed how important it is for faculty to create a context in which learners can reconstruct their understanding of the world and engage in discovery learning. This work of reconstructing would be based on their own experience. In discovery learning students are not given the facts or information but are required to find things out for themselves. Dewey and Vygotsky, in particular, focused on the social nature of learning.

Small-Group Theory

Cooperative learning is grounded in social psychology as articulated in the 1940s by Kurt Lewin and Martin Deutsch, who were fascinated by the nature and power of small-group theory. Together with educational psychology, small-group theory is the basis for the cooperative-learning movement initiated by David Johnson and Roger Johnson at the University of Minnesota and by R. Slavin at Johns Hopkins University.

In the past two decades other champions of cooperative learning have appeared on the educational scene. At the City University of New York, Kenneth Bruffee and his associates have used strategies for enabling undergraduates to work on their thinking or writing out loud with one another. This has led to a peer-writing approach that has changed the writing class into an active workshop where writers work on their writing with other writers.

Epistemological Theory

Recent research in social constructionism and in feminist theory and pedagogy gives a philosophical rationale for those who structure their

College Classes: A Range of Options for Faculty (San Francisco: Jossey-Bass Publishers, 1996); and Liz Beaty, *Action Learning: A Guide for Professional, Management and Educational Development*, Second Edition, (London: Kogan Page, 1995).

classrooms around cooperative learning. Social constructionists assert that knowledge is socially constructed by communities of individuals, i.e., by successive conversations in ever-changing political and social environments. Theorists in feminist pedagogy argue that students are diverse learners whose *Weltanschauung* is shaped by their gender, race, age, cultural experience, and class. They are on the opposite end of the spectrum from those who assume that students are a uniform body of isolated individuals ready to receive knowledge through uniform modes of information delivery. The former strive to help students learn to synthesize the material themselves and develop their capacity to think.

Why Cooperative Learning?
We know more about cooperative learning than we do about the use of technology in education, the efficacy of lectures, or almost any other facet of education. Many studies have shown that students working in small groups learn content better and retain it longer than when the same material is presented in other instructional formats. Moreover, regardless of the subject matter, students who work in small, cooperative groups express a high level of satisfaction with their classes.

Research suggests that collaborative learning facilitates the development of students' higher-order thinking skills.[2] Small groups of peers working together offer their members affective and cognitive support while solving complex and challenging problems. Students working in small groups are motivated to try new learning strategies and learn to think critically when they hear peers raise questions, wrestle with situations, and deal with uncertainty.

Students feel isolated in many classes, particularly at large public universities. They need to make contact with their peers and often do not know how to do so. Cooperative learning groups provide a venue for students to make contact with their peers in a structured environment. Such groups also force students to take an active part in the class. It is virtually impossible to adopt the role of a spectator in them. And because cooperative learning groups are small, optimally four students, even shy students feel comfortable speaking out. Interaction with peers shakes students from an egocentric perspective. It exposes them to new and differing viewpoints and encourages them to take risks, question assumptions, and create new knowledge. Through interaction students learn the interpersonal skills they need to understand how knowledge is generated in academic disciplines, business, and other fields. Coopera-

[2] Kate Sandberg, "Collaborative Learning and Critical Thinking," in *The Critical Writing Workshop: Designing Writing Assignments to Foster Critical Thinking* ed. Toni-Lee Capossela (Portsmouth, New Hampshire: Boynton Cook, 1993) 143.

tive learning may make difficult assignments easier and even make them fun because there is a support group working on a common endeavor. Cooperative groups foster positive interdependence: students share goals, resources, and rewards. Students in these groups must believe that they cannot succeed unless the group as a whole succeeds. At the same time, the feedback such structures allow encourages individual accountability.[3]

Cooperative Learning and Critical Thinking

How does cooperative learning influence critical thinking? First, small-group discussion is superior to lectures in improving thinking and problem solving. Second, cooperative learning explicitly emphasizes problem-solving procedures in various in-class exercises, as will be seen in the final chapter of this book. Third, cooperative learning increases attention to metacognition because the latter occurs as a matter of course in group processing. For example, in cooperative learning groups one student is assigned the role of reflector. The role of the reflective is metacognitive in nature because the reflector has to think about the implications of the learning process and write a report about this for the group.

Face-to-Face Promotive Interaction

Promotive interaction occurs when students help each other learn. When students are put into learning groups they automatically help each other learn by sharing information. If one person in the group has attended a course with me before, he or she knows what I want and is able to tell other group members about the demands of a particular assignment.

In other words, promotive interaction deals with individuals working together in harmony so as to turn out a superior product. Face-to-face promotive interaction occurs when students help one another learn. They may give one another feedback on their work or performance. Or they may exchange materials, slides, charts, maps, and other instructional resources.[4]

For example, in my classes architecture and veterinary medicine students have access to specialized libraries and thus have the opportunity to share resources not available to all students. Although promotive interaction involves students challenging one another's reasoning and conclusions, an equally important aspect involves students acting to-

---

3 David W. Johnson and Roger T. Johnson, *Learning Together and Alone: Cooperative, Competitive and Individualistic Learning* (Boston: Allyn and Bacon, 1987) 23. One may begin cooperative learning by asking students to design an ideal classroom. See Steven Levy, *Staring from Scratch: One Classroom Builds Its Own Curriculum* (Portsmouth, N.H.: Heinemann, 1996), 40–64.

4 Ibid., 54.

ward one another in trusting and trustworthy ways. To be trustworthy means to respond to another person's risk-taking in a way that ensures that the other person will experience beneficial consequences.

I encourage trust in two ways: first, by modeling trustworthy behavior in my interactions with the class as a whole. Second, I teach students social skills that help them work effectively in a group setting. Students are as capable of obstructing one another's learning as they are of supporting it, but in cooperative learning students know that turning out a quality product requires everyone's effort. They help each other learn by sharing information, and they come to feel responsible for one another. Promotive interaction allows them to discuss issues and challenge suppositions and conclusions at the same time as they help to create a safe and supportive environment in which to do this.

Group Processing

In contradistinction to traditional learning groups, cooperative learning groups engage in group processing. In fact, one member of the group, the reflector, keeps a running account of the group's progress in terms of process. Processing also occurs in the class as a whole: the facilitator gives feedback on how well each group is working together.[5]

Successful processing encompasses several elements. Allow sufficient time for group processing to occur. My rule of thumb is that we will not engage in an in-class group exercise without allowing time for processing the experience. Without this experience students will fail to see the metacognitive implications of the exercise. In my Introduction to Religion class, for instance, I have a segment on ethical decision making. I ask students to stand on either side of the class depending on their answer to these questions: What kind of food do you prefer, fast food or haute cuisine? What kind of car do you prefer, a small, gas-efficient auto like the Ford Escort or a large gas guzzler like a Cadillac? Students are not allowed to stand in the middle of the class but must decide between the two types of food and vehicles. After several similar questions I have the class members sit down and process the experience. In this exercise, they get in touch with the values they hold dear. I then point out that they must be willing to stand up for their values and affirm them in a public way. I ask students what they learned about themselves from doing this exercise.

In processing what a cooperative learning group accomplished during a class period, the instructor must ask specific questions rather than vague ones, e.g., what conclusions did your group come to or what

5 Wendy Duncan-Hewitt, David L. Mount, Dan Apple, *A Handbook on Cooperative Learning* 2 ed. (Corvallis, OR: Pacific Crest Software, Inc. 1995) 17.

insight did your group arrive at in today's discussion? I find it best to periodically change the questions I ask in order for the groups to focus their reflections. By varying the format of group processing, it is easy to maintain students' involvement in the processing.

Social Skills

Cooperative learning does not just happen. Students do not sit at the same table and work on their assignments individually. Instead they must be explicitly taught how to work together successfully with their peers. Many students have never worked in cooperative learning groups and will need practice in such interpersonal skills as active listening, giving and receiving constructive criticism, and the use of "I" messages.

In cooperative learning groups students learn both academic subject matter (taskwork) and small-group skills they will need to function as part of a group (teamwork). The taskwork cannot be done if students do not learn the teamwork skills. Johnson and Johnson call the small-group skills the engine that powers cooperative learning groups. Cooperative learning groups will not be effective without good communication, effective leadership, trust among the group members, and constructive conflict resolution.[6]

Teaching Cooperative Skills

There are several steps to take to ensure that students learn these skills.

Step 1.   Ask class members what social skills they will need to cooperate effectively with their peers. Students must see the need for the skill in order to be motivated to learn it.

Step 2.   Demonstrate the skill and describe it step by step so that students clearly understand it. Point out good models in other students or ask the class to identify a student who has mastered that particular skill.

Step 3.   Organize practice sessions so that students receive feedback on how well they are practicing the skill. The feedback should be immediate, specific, and frequent. It is needed in order to identify progress in the mastery of a skill and to correct errors.[7]

---

6 David W. Johnson and Roger T. Johnson, 186.

7 Ibid., 188. To see how cooperative learning interacts differently within the various aspects of the learning process, see Robert J. Marzano, "The Many Faces of Cooperation Across the Dimensions of Learning," in *Enhancing Thinking Through Cooperative Learning*, Neil Davidson and Toni Worsham, eds., (N.Y. and London: Teachers College Press, 1992), 7–28.

Step 4.   Have students use the skill throughout the course so that it becomes second nature to them. In other words the skill must be integrated into the students' behavioral repertoire so that its use becomes automatic and natural.

Step 5.   Classroom norms must support the use of the skill. Faculty need to model the skills themselves and reward students for using the skills by, for instance, congratulating them in public for using the skill. Faculty must demonstrate to students that they value the use of these skills.

Teaching Communication Skills

Communication may be understood as a meeting of minds or a meeting of meanings. It refers to all those symbols and clues used by persons in giving and receiving meaning. Communication is both complex and incomplete. In addition to using words, one communicates through gestures, body movements, tone of voice, and facial expressions. There are two main categories of communication skills: sending and receiving.[8]

Sending Skills

Important sending skills include clearly communicating ideas and feelings. Students do this by using "I" messages in which they own their message, letting others know what their thoughts and feelings really are. If class members use such expressions as "our group," "some people," or "most people," it is difficult to know what they really feel and think. Those who communicate well firmly state their case, can clarify what they say, are able to ask for feedback, and are receptive to feedback when they receive it. The dysfunctional communicator, on the other hand, sends incomplete messages, may dismiss requests to clarify, and leaves the receiver guessing about what's inside his or her mind. For example, a wife wants her husband to see a movie with her. If she communicates functionally she might say, "John, let's see the movie *Sense and Sensibility* tonight." If she communicates dysfunctionally, she might say, "John, you would like to see a movie tonight," "It would do you good to see a movie, John," or "We might as well see a movie. There's nothing else to do."[9]

Clearly, a message must be complete and specific; that is, assumptions, intentions, frame of reference, or leaps in thinking must be explicit. If they are not, the listener will hear the words but not the full message. Similarly, verbal and nonverbal messages must be congruent.

---

[8] Virigina Satir, *Conjoint Family Therapy* (Palo Alto, California: Science and Behavior Books, Inc. 1967) 63 ff.

[9] Ibid., 67.

Problems in communication may arise when verbal messages do not match nonverbal ones. I had, for instance, a professor who smiled in class when he was upset. The mixed messages his behavior sent made it difficult for students to know his state of mind.

Finally, receivers should provide feedback concerning the way messages are being received. As a rule, I ask students on an individual basis how they are doing in my class. That way I find out how I'm teaching.

Receiving Skills

A major barrier to good communication is this: many people approve of, disapprove of, or otherwise skew the message they are receiving. A concrete receiving skill is the ability to paraphrase, or to restate a point or statement for clarity and to demonstrate the listener's comprehension. A good paraphrase restates the sender's remarks in new words and uses such expressions as "Your position is . . . ," "You feel that . . . ," or "You think. . . ." A paraphrase should avoid indications of approval or disapproval and state exactly what the sender said without adding or subtracting from the message. I often use paraphrasing when a student makes a complex statement that is hard to summarize, and I always ask if I have captured the essence of his or her remarks.[10]

Have you ever walked into a classroom where the students seem to be lethargic, passive, and tired? I have, and to determine whether I am correct in my intuition, I share my perception with the class and ask if I am on target. Frequently, I am and that tells me that I must do something out of the ordinary to wake up the class. A perception check may also be done with an individual student. A student may make a statement in class that is unclear. It is then appropriate to ask, "What I think you mean is. . . . Am I correct in this?" The process, not the actual words used, is important in trying to negotiate meaning.

Creating a Positive Environment

The first few days of class are critical in building a sense of community in the classroom.[11] I always plan an activity that provides opportunities for students to solve problems together or to speak to one another at the start of a course. Students also respond if I take an interest in them as individuals rather than see them as anonymous faces in a crowd, so I make an effort to learn their names, as well as to have them learn each

10 Robert R. Carkhuff, *The Art of Helping: A Guide for Developing Helping Skills for Parents, Teachers and Counselors* (Amherst, Mass.: Human Resource Development Press, 1973) 65.

11 Barbara Gross Davis, 20 ff. On organizing an interactive learning environment, see Dennis Adams and Mary Hamm, *New Designs for Teaching and Learning: Promoting Active Learning in Tomorrow's Schools* (San Francisco: Jossey Bass Publishers, 1994), 49–55.

other's names. I also distribute a list of principles on which we will base our interactions:

1. I am critical of ideas, not of people.
2. I listen to all ideas even if I do not always agree with them.
3. I restate what others have said if it is not clear to me.
4. I endeavor to look at all sides of a question.
5. I am interested in arriving at the best decision possible for my group, rather than with trying to look good myself.
6. I change my mind when the evidence indicates that I should.

Finally, I give students written contracts that state their obligations to their group and deadlines for the completion of tasks. Committing instructions to writing serves as a concrete reminder to students, and a written contract has an air of finality that an oral statement can lack.

Two general strategies help maximize cooperative learning:

1. Plan Carefully   There are three general types of group work: (1) formal learning groups, (2) informal learning groups, and (3) study teams.[12] **Formal learning groups** are set up to complete such specific tasks as carry out a project or write a group position paper. Groups may finish their task in one class period or in several. **Informal learning groups** are ad hoc groups of students established to solve a problem or ask a question within a single class session. I use them to provide a change of pace, to give students the opportunity to reflect on what they are learning, and to see how well students have understood the material. **Study teams** are set up for the entire semester or quarter. They have a stable membership and allow members to assist, encourage, and support one another in fulfilling course requirements. When someone has missed a class period, members of the study team inform the absent member what transpired in the class. In my classes I use both formal learning groups and informal learning groups. The formal learning groups last all semester and incorporate the role of study teams as mentioned above.

Decide which projects, topics, or themes will lend themselves to formal and informal learning groups as you map out your course syllabus. Assign students to specific groups of four each. Groups with fewer than four members lack critical mass, and larger groups mean that assignments will take longer to complete. It is important that you make the group assignments. Students are very likely to pick a safe group, or one in which they already know someone. They are also less likely to get a good mix. As you choose the groups, try to balance them in terms of male, female, white, and minority students.

12 David W. Johnson and Roger T. Johnson, 100.

Once the groups have been decided upon, do not change them even if a particular group has trouble getting along. Otherwise, students will not learn the skills needed to resolve conflict. This is what students will face in the real world, whether they find themselves in business, industry, education, or any other field, and it is important that they learn how to get along now.

Explain in your course syllabus and tell the students on the first day of class that this class will be different. State explicitly that you will use cooperative learning in which students are put into small groups of four to work on assignments in class. Students who feel uncomfortable with the cooperative learning format can drop the class at once, and those who remain will know from day one what is expected of them.

2. Explain very carefully, preferably in writing and orally, how the groups will operate. I find it best to restate several times exactly what the learning groups are supposed to accomplish. Students will often unwittingly tune you out the first time around, or they will be nervous about working in a small group and their anxiety will prevent them from hearing your instructions. After stating the objectives, ask a student to restate— or paraphrase—them for the class.

Role Playing
It is very important to assign students a particular role in the cooperative learning group. These are the four roles I use in my cooperative learning groups:

1. The *team captain* has the task of keeping the group on task and focused. He or she is involved in the work of the group, reads the assignment to the group, and mediates conflict. The captain also manages time and keeps the process flowing.
2. The *recorder* takes minutes on the work of the group and writes down the salient points. He or she serves as spokesperson for the group in reporting back to the class as a whole.
3. The *encourager* gives team members positive feedback on their work and encourages them to share their ideas and feelings. The encourager has the task of getting the most out of the group.
4. The *reflector* is concerned with group process rather than product. The reflector's job is the hardest because he or she must note the strengths and weaknesses of the group and provide insight into its dynamics. For example, the reflector may comment on the fact that

the group lacked direction at first and then became clear about what it wanted to accomplish.[13]

If a group has five members, the recorder's job can be divided so that one student keeps minutes and the other makes reports.

It is important that students play each of the four roles at some point during the term. Initially, students may resist rotating roles within the group, but it is up to the teacher as facilitator to see that this is done.

The Role of Discussion in Cooperative Learning

In cooperative learning most of the time will be spent in either small- or large-group discussions. Hence I offer some advice on encouraging student participation in discussion and in leading a discussion.

Be Explicit About Your Expectations

Both in your syllabus and on the first day of class comment on the role discussion will play in the course. Tell students, for example, that you expect everyone to participate in discussions, that the class is a "safe haven" to explore and test new ideas and to react to new and fresh thinking.

In my classes I have a "smile and pass" rule. If I call on a student by name and that student declines to answer for whatever reason, the student may simply smile and pass. This rule allows me to call back to reality students who are day-dreaming, but it is not threatening to students who feel on the spot when they are called on by name and do not know the answer. No one enjoys admitting ignorance, and the "smile and pass" rule gives students a graceful way out.

Some faculty ask students who do not wish to be called on in class to put their names on a sheet of paper. The instructor puts a star next to their name as a reminder to skip over them. Faculty who do this find that few students use this option and some even change their mind during the semester.[14]

Prepare Students for a Discussion

There are several strategies that are appropriate for helping students prepare for a discussion. I have used the following ones with good success.

---

13 Wendy Duncan-Hewitt et al., 15. For tips on implementation, see James L. Cooper, et al, "Cooperative Learning in the Classroom," in Changing College Classrooms: New Teaching and Learning Strategies for an Increasingly Complex World Diane F. Halpern and Associates, eds. (San Francisco: Jossey-Bass Publishers, 1994), 82–84.

14 Barbara Gross Davis, 64.

Give students the following form for reading assignments that will be discussed in class:

NAME _____   DATE: _____

Before Reading:
1. What previous knowledge do you have about this topic/reading?
2. Why are you doing this reading, apart from the fact that it has been assigned to you?

While Reading:
1. List the unfamiliar terms you find in this reading.
2. What questions does this reading raise?

After Reading:
1. What is the author's thesis or main argument?
2. How does this reading fit in with the purpose of the course?
3. How does this reading relate to your life?[15]

The answers to these questions provide an excellent point of departure for discussion. You might also have students prepare a one-hundred word position piece or a list of questions they would like to hear discussed. Another idea is to assign a weekly reaction paper of one to two pages on a specific topic. Again, these papers can serve as the basis for a class discussion.

Beginning a Discussion

To minimize students' fears of speaking up, ask them to come up with the dumbest question they can think of based on the assigned readings for the day. This strategy unleashes students' creativity and spirit of playfulness. After they have been asked this question several times, students make it a game as the class sifts through the questions and focuses on the good ones.[16]

You may also begin the discussion by asking students to volunteer a memorable event in their own lives that relates to the reading under discussion. Explore both the points in common and the differences and connect the discussion to the readings.

On occasion I have taken one or two students aside after a class session and asked them to come to the next class with a provocative question based on the reading. I have also asked students to provide a

[15] Sarah M. Carroll and Daniel K. Apple, *Learning Assessment Journal* (Corvallis, OR: Pacific Crest Software, Inc., 1995) 15.
[16] Barbara Gross Davis, 67.

rationale for why they want to hear the question discussed. I usually select students I know to be outspoken when I first give this assignment.

Ask a Controversial Question
Group students into informal learning groups based on the pro/con position they take. Direct the groups to construct two to three arguments to support their position. By writing each group's statements on the board (if the class is relatively small, i.e., up to 35 students), the way is paved for a general discussion that can really take off.

Hints on Guiding a Discussion
After about twenty minutes of group discussion, I ask the team recorders to summarize what their group said. This often leads to a good discussion when groups have come to different conclusions about the material under consideration. To vary the format, I often ask for a reflector's report from each group. This ensures that the group is doing both reports (the recorder's and the reflector's) because I never tell students ahead of time which report I want to hear.

Maintaining Focus
You can list the day's issues and questions on the board so all can see and hand out written lists of the questions you want each group to discuss on a particular day, but what do you do when the discussion goes off on a tangent? Immediately stop and describe exactly what has been occurring. I interject comments like these: "Peter, what you say is very enlightening and even provocative, but we also need to get back to the original question, which is. . . ." Or I may say something like this: "Mary, your point is well taken, but does this apply to the question of God's existence?"

I like to jot down the main points that emerge from the discussion and refer to them when summarizing students' comments. You may also write down problem areas that need clarification or point out the implications of what students have said. If students are way off base, clarify confusing information by saying, "I'd like to clear up a misunderstanding before we continue."

What should be done if the discussion becomes heated? I find it easy to defuse the situation with a calm remark such as "Time out. It's not fair when three people jump all over a classmate. Let's give Becky a chance to state her views." Or "we need to identify points of agreement and points of disagreement." It may suffice to say, "This discussion is becoming too emotional. Let's slow down a minute." Or "I'm afraid this discussion is leading nowhere. Let's move on to a new question."

Other ways to calm a discussion are these: ask abstract or theoretical questions, avoid calling on specific individuals, slow the tempo of one's voice, and ask students to raise their hands before they speak. Certain non-verbal clues indicate that a discussion is not going very well: private conversations, lack of participation, excessive hair splitting, students lining up on sides and refusing to compromise, the same points are being repeated. Take a direct approach and ask students why they think the discussion seems to be breaking down. They can be quite candid in their remarks.[17]

You may introduce a new topic in order to jump-start a discussion. Or ask very specific questions and call on students known for their strong opinions. Beware of cutting off discussion too early. A certain amount of disagreement can be helpful because it stimulates thought. You may even generate a good discussion by saying, "Who can argue the opposite point of view?"

Ending the Discussion
I like to select two or three students at the start of the large-group discussion to give a summation at the end of the class. Tell the class at the start of the discussion that someone will be called upon at the end to summarize the discussion in terms of major issues and conclusions. This certainly motivates class members to listen to the discussion because they may be called upon to give a summation.

I like to thank those who participated in the discussion for their willingness to speak up and put themselves on the line. At times, I may summarize the discussion myself, pointing out jumping off points for the next group discussion. If the discussion ends and there is still class time remaining, I ask students to jot down in their notebooks one question that is uppermost in their minds. Students turn in these questions anonymously, and they form the basis of the next class session.

How to Evaluate a Discussion
There are several way to evaluate a discussion. Require students to write a paragraph or two in which they place the discussion in the context of issues previously discussed in class. Then break the students into groups of two to discuss what they wrote. An alternative is to have students share their paragraphs within their cooperative learning group. Or ask students to process the large-group discussion in terms of questions like these:

— Did the discussion stay on the topic?
— Did the discussion make you re-think your assumptions or point of view?

17 Ibid., 71.

— Give some instances of particularly insightful comments made during the discussion.
— Who requested information, solicited ideas, or invited reactions?
— Who clarified the discussion by suggesting alternative ways of viewing the problem or restating the contribution of others?
— Did anyone raise his or her hand to speak and was not called on?

The Role of the Instructor

The instructor must specify the instructional objectives for the cooperative learning groups. For each lesson it is necessary to specify both an academic and a social-skills objective.[18] The academic objective must be specified at the correct level for the students. This may be difficult to do at times because faculty are removed from their lives as students and may find it difficult to remember what it was like to be a student. For instance, I once taught a class on twentieth-century religious thought to thirty undergraduates using *Dietrich Bonhoeffer: Witness to Jesus Christ*, edited by John de Gruchy, as one of my texts. There were many foreign words, both Latin and German, in the text, which heightened the anxiety level of my students. I was not bothered by these foreign terms, but they made my students very anxious. I did not realize how difficult the course was for my students until I gave the first quiz and realized I needed to scale down my expectations. To nurture their self-confidence, I allowed them to make up the second quiz themselves. This helped their grades and allowed me to assess their level and then determine what I needed to do.

The instructor must also specify what small-group skills will be stressed during the lesson. It is easy for instructors to skip the social-skills objectives, but they are greatly needed to train students to work together. Here are some examples of what I do to specify learning objectives for small-group skills.

1. I tell students that today we will emphasize listening skills. Before they make a comment, they must practice summarizing the point made by the person who spoke before them.
2. In order to ensure that groups process how well they are achieving their goals and sustaining good working relationships among members, I have them answer two questions at the end of the period: "What did each member do that was helpful for the group?" and "What could each member do to improve the working of the group?"[19]

[18] David W. Johnson and Roger T. Johnson, 103.
[19] Ibid., 117.

Accountability
In my classes when the group does an assignment or project an individual grade is given to each student. After the group is assigned a task and roles are chosen by the group members, I often ask for a report from the recorder or from the reflector on the progress of the group. Students know that I will call on them at random, and they want to be able to make a good report rather than look foolish in front of their peers. If a student is struggling to give a decent report, I ask him or her to take a few minutes to work on it and then check back later in the class.

There are several way to structure individual accountability in a small group. The instructor should monitor the pattern of participation found in the group. I do this by going from group to group and taking notes on their interactions. One may also give practice tests, select members at random to explain their answers to a question, or have group members edit one another's work. Another good way to structure individual accountability is to have students teach what they know to someone else or to use what they have learned on a different problem.[20]

On Making Interventions
As a rule I do not intervene in a group except when absolutely necessary. Cooperative learning groups should solve their own problems. I recently observed a group of four deal with a student who was extremely dogmatic. I knew from a previous classes that this student held to his views like a bulldog. My inclination was to intervene when the group met an impasse caused by this student. I waited, though, and the group was strong enough to solve its own problem. If one feels compelled to intervene, try asking the group to create three possible solutions to the problem and use those as a basis for action.

I do find it appropriate, however, to intervene to assist the group with its task. In this case your interventions should be specific to the assignment. Instead of saying, for instance, "That's the right answer," say "That's one possible way of leading the class in Buddhist meditation." You can reinforce the desired learning by using very specific questions: "What are you doing and why? And how will this help you?"

Some Problem Areas
Some conflict is inevitable in cooperative learning groups. In fact, a lack of conflict may be a sign not of harmony but of apathy. Conflicts that are managed in a constructive manner are a source of delight, fun, and creativity. They also provide the opportunity to engage in higher-order thinking. If managed in a destructive fashion, conflicts cause division,

[20] Barbara Gross Davis, 153.

anxiety, and frustration, and even bitterness, so it is vital that students be given the skills to manage conflicts constructively.

Students as Peacemakers

Students must be given the skills to negotiate constructive resolutions to their conflicts. This involves several steps.[21]

1. Students need to define the conflict, e.g., "I want to do my report on the Sufi mystics and you chose the same topic."
2. Students should state how they feel: "I'm disappointed we both can't work on the same topic."
3. They should be able to offer reasons for how they feel: "I already know a lot about Zen, and if I have to choose another topic I may get a bad grade."
4. Students should be able to summarize their understanding of what the other person feels and wants and the reasons for this.
5. Students should be able to devise three alternative plans to solve the problem/conflict.
6. Students should be able to find a compromise both sides can live with.

Students as Mediators

Mediation refers to the processes of bringing about reconciliation or agreement between opponents in a dispute. I teach students how to help their peers negotiate a constructive resolution to their conflicts. After introducing her- or himself to the group, the mediator ascertains whether or not the students want to solve the dispute. If they say no, mediation is impossible. If they both assent to mediation, the mediator runs through the guidelines:

1. I will not take sides in the dispute or determine who is right or wrong. I will, instead, decide how you can solve the conflict.
2. I will assist you in finding a solution that both of you find acceptable.
3. Each of you will state his or her view of the conflict without interruption.
4. The rules are these: no name calling, be totally honest, you must abide by a solution if you agree to it, and everything you say is confidential.[22]

---

21 David W. Johnson and Roger T. Johnson, 232.
22 Ibid., 233.

The Steps of Negotiation

The mediator determines what the parties feel, what they want, and their reasons for feeling as they do. The parties reverse perspectives, putting themselves into the other side's position. They come up with three optional agreements and finally they reach agreement. The mediator checks the next day to ensure that the agreement is working. If it is not working, the process of mediation is repeated.

Students practice mediation skills until they become second nature. The instructor selects two students to serve as official mediators who will help resolve any conflicts that occur in the small groups. The role of mediator is rotated throughout the class so that every student has an opportunity to play that role. Once-a-week refresher lessons are given by the instructor. The great thing about mediation is this: it allows students to make decisions about issues that affect their lives rather than having a decision imposed on them by the instructor. Students also learn a skill for life.

Students as Creatures of Habit

Be patient with yourself as you experiment with cooperative learning. It may take years to become an expert, and you will undoubtedly meet student resistance. By the time they are in your class, students have had almost twenty years of working competitively and individualistically and will be unaccustomed to working together. They may feel insecure and anxious, and you, as the instructor, should openly acknowledge their anger, anxiety, insecurity, and concern and help them find the source of these emotions. For the first couple of days allow the groups to engage in team-building activities, giving them time for discovery, learning, and reflection. Tell them that stress and frustration are intrinsic to the learning process and should be expected.[23]

As you go from group to group, spend time monitoring those groups that are experiencing problems. Give more time to complete a task if the group needs it and less time if you need to increase the pressure. Students may become overconfident if the instructor is too soft, but the group may give up if its members experience too much frustration and failure. The instructor's role is to find the via media between these two extremes. It will try your patience and your creativity as you attempt to create work for the group and to come up with an academic and a social-skills objective for each class, but it is well worth the effort for you and your students.

---

[23] Wendy Duncan-Hewitt *et al.*, 82 ff.

Summary

In this chapter we offered a definition of cooperative learning and tried to shed some light on its historical roots. Cooperative learning does not just happen in the classroom. Students must be prepared for cooperative learning and that means they need to be given the requisite skills to do so. These skills are largely communication skills such as communicating clearly, listening perceptively, paraphrasing what another group member has said, and doing a perception check.

This chapter has given some hints on how faculty in religious studies can give their students the skills required to work cooperatively in a small group. The role of discussion in cooperative learning has been given particular attention in this chapter. At the end of this chapter we have noted some problem areas in trying to implement cooperative learning in the religious studies' curriculum.

In the next chapter we will look at the relationship betwen creativity and critical thinking. To this end we now turn.

6

CREATIVITY AND CRITICAL THINKING

"The creative mind is like a parachute: it has to be opened to be of any use."

Anonymous

This chapter begins with a brief look at the barriers to teaching creatively and a discussion of the nature of creativity. Although creativity and critical thinking may be distinguished, my research has led me to stress their overlap, and this chapter will offer practical classroom applications for encouraging and enhancing both. Special attention is given to intuitive techniques that can be used effectively in religious studies, such as map-making, imagery, brainstorming, analogies, centering prayer, intuition, and meditation. These techniques may be modified to fit practically any course in the academic study of religion.

Barriers to Creative Teaching
According to one educational psychologist, creativity means that special quality in students that faculty in *other* classrooms stifle.[1] Instructors who are authoritarian, rigid, and dependent solely on the lecture method stifle their students' creative spirit by demanding total conformity. For a host of reasons, faculty cultivate these qualities—and avoid creative teaching. Certainly one of the most compelling reasons is the fear of censure. As we have discussed in an earlier chapter, new faculty are reluctant to explore new teaching methods for fear of censure either by their department head or by their peers when they come up before the twin gods of promotion and tenure. We know that traditional teaching methods will be recognized and accepted—and are probably more likely to be rewarded. Hence we go with the tried and true. As teachers, we are also afraid of failing. We do not want to embarrass ourselves, or as the Italians say, cut a *bruta figura*, in trying out new pedagogical tools. Nor do we want to risk alienating students.

Engaging in new behavior always involves a certain amount of risk-taking and nerve, and the classroom is not exempt from such laws of

---

[1] Guy R. Lefran'cois, *Psychology for Teaching: A Bear Always Faces the Front* (Belmont, Calif., Wadsworth Publ. Co., 1975), 251.

human nature. The fear of failure leads us to reject many ideas, but we are equally victims of the myth of the "one right way." Traditionally, psychologists associate the right brain and its activity with such creative behavior as visualizing and generating ideas. The left brain controls judicial thought, which chooses, compares, and analyzes. Although we think both creatively and judicially, more than 90 percent of formal education deals with judicial thinking. As youngsters we are taught the "one right way" to solve a problem. Hence judgment increases with age while our creativity withers.[2]

The Nature of Creativity

My wife and I recently bought a handsomely decorated house. Our bedside lamp, however, did not match the decor of our new master bedroom. What were we to do? Replace the lamp with a color that matched or replace the wallpaper? My wife sewed an off-white cloth garment around the lamp so that it fit the decor of the bedroom wonderfully. That, I submit, is an example of creativity.

For years, literally millions of vehicles traveled through the Holland and Lincoln tunnels and across the Bayonne and Verazzano bridges connecting Brooklyn and Staten Island, New York. Drivers paid tolls going in and coming out, resulting in major traffic tie-ups in both directions. Then someone had the bright idea to charge a toll (double the cost of a one-way fee) only on the way out. This creative idea reduced the traffic congestion by half.

Creativity vs. Creating

These examples bring us to the question of the nature of creativity. People are creative for different reasons and in sundry ways. And they are creative to different degrees. David Perkins, a leading researcher in the area of creativity, distinguishes between creativity and creating. *Creativity* involves traits that make one creative. To *create*, on the other hand, is to call upon many resources, not all of which are intrinsically creative.[3]

---

[2] James R. Evans, *Creative Thinking in the Decision and Management Sciences* (Cincinnati: South-Western Publ. Co., 1990), 47. See the excellent discussion on creative insight skills in Robert J. Sternberg and Louise Spear-Swerling, *Teaching For Thinking* (Washington, D.C.: American Psychological Association, 1996), 83–100; Robert J. Sternberg and J. E. Davidson, eds., *The Nature of Insight* (Cambridge, MA: MIT Press, 1995); Robert J. Sternberg and T. I. Lubart, *Defying the Crowd: Cultivating Creativity in a Culture of Conformity* (New York: Free Press, 1995); and Diane F. Halpern, *Thought and Knowledge: An Introduction to Critical Thinking* Third Edition, Mahwah, N.J.: Lawrence Erlbaum Associates, Publishers, 1996), 365–392.

[3] D. N. Perkins, *The Mind's Best Work* (Cambridge, MA: Harvard University Press, 1981), 275. See D. N. Perkins, "The Nature and Nurture of Creativity," in *Dimensions of Thinking and Cognitive Instruction*, eds. Beau Fly Jones and Lorna Idol (Hillsdale, New Jersey: Lawrence Erlbaum Associates, Publishers, 1990), p. 422. See Frank E. Williams, "Intellectual

Creating is a process of gradually selecting an actual product from an infinite number of possibilities. Because of its unique components, creating transcends what a person can do effortlessly. Creating demands 1) planning—which may involve blueprints, outlines, and spontaneous ideas. These in turn involve selection. Plans arise by abstracting from particulars, and planning entails noticing opportunities and detecting flaws. Creating also involves 2) undoing, which means being able to set a work aside and redo it, allowing for mistakes and corrections. Creating requires 3) making means into ends: the creator or maker often addresses a means as an end in itself, instead of being preoccupied with the final product. Creating also demands 4) purpose. This means creating or solving problems that require invention.

In spite of Perkins's distinction, the similarities between creativity and creating outweigh their differences. In creating a product we use many resources not intrinsically creative. However, the way the resources are put together may be creative. To distinguish thus sharply between creativity and creating is tantamount to splitting hairs. We may, however, distinguish between the outer and the inner nature of creativity. The outer nature of creativity concerns results. The inner nature of creativity may be known only indirectly.[4]

The Inner Nature of Creative Thinking
Psychologists note three ways of thinking about the inner nature of creative thinking. First, there is "potency." Some researchers believe that creative thinking depends on the power to generate original appropriate ideas. If we can measure this power, we can measure a person's potential to think creatively. Psychologists speak about "ideational fluency," or the ability to generate quickly a large number of appropriate ideas, and "ideational flexibility," or the ability to generate varied uses for an object. You may be able to come up with any number of uses for a brick, but if they all employ a brick as a weight, they do not show great flexibility.

In point of fact, real-world creative achievement does not correlate with the measure of ideational fluency and ideational flexibility.[5] A person may be able to generate quickly a lot of ideas (ideational fluency) or may be able to generate varied uses for an object (ideational flexi-

Creativity and the Teacher," *Journal of Creative Behavior* I, No. 2, (Spring 1967): 174–176. For a definition of creativity, see Richard Penaskovic, "Toward a Definition of Creativity," in *Essays on Creativity and Science* (Honolulu: Hawaii Council of Teachers of English, 1986), 102–108.

4 Perkins, 471.

5 Perkins, 418. See Frank Barron, *Creativity And Personal Freedom* (New York: D. Van Nostrand Company, 1968), 239.

bility), but these qualities alone are not enough. A better measure of a person's creativity is his or her ability to produce quality work, like a Karl Barth or a Karl Rahner.

Second, some researchers suggest that creative thinking may reflect specific patterns of thought. Creative thinkers are distinguished by their extensive search for problems worth solving and for their flexibility in defining problems. Do inventive people think in opposites, bringing disparate ideas or concepts together in a new synthesis? Only rarely has research identified a relationship between patterns of thinking and a person's creativity.[6]

Finally, psychologists find that creative thinking may reflect values. Creative individuals have a high tolerance for ambiguity and have intrinsic motivation in valuing their research. In other words, they value their work for its own sake, rather than for such extrinsic rewards as money. Furthermore, creativity does seem to emerge because an individual is trying to be creative. In short, research suggests that creating is an intentional endeavor dictated by one's values.[7]

Creativity, Originality, and Imagination
Are creative works discontinuous with the past? Do they involve a radical break with the tradition? The answer to both questions is no. Even in the case of revolutionary innovations, continuities and connections with the tradition are always present. This must be the case insofar as such innovations can only be understood in the light of such traditions. As Sharon Bailin observes, the originality of created products is valued primarily because it provides the possibility for new kinds of solutions to existing problems and new directions for research.[8]

Creativity should not be thought of as a highly mysterious, irrational process. Rather, it involves the excellent use of our ordinary thinking processes to produce outstanding products. The creative process itself does not differ from our ordinary thought processes, and the knowledge, skills, and rules of a discipline play a central role in creativity. Such skills require flexibility, the need for constant revision, and, of course, considerable thought. The creative person has mastered such skills, which allows him or her the freedom to work and to make original contributions to a particular area or discipline.[9] Creativity and imagination are

6 Perkins, 421. For an excellent discussion of reading and writing as design, see David N. Perkins, *Knowledge As Design* (Hillsdale, N.J.: Lawrence Erlbaum Associates, Publishers, 1986), 64–92.

7 Perkins, 422.

8 Sharon Bailin, *Achieving Extraordinary Ends: An Essay on Creativity* (Dordrecht, The Netherlands, Kluwer Publications, 1988), 31.

9 Bailin, 85.

the cream of thinking. Imagination, or transcending the given with new ideas and generating possibilities, shows itself in the execution of a skilled performance. Both our thinking in general and the skills we possess are charged with imagination. To be creative means to transcend the confines of convention in an imaginative way.[10]

Defining Creativity

Creativity may refer to an individual's potential for achievement. Social scientists assert that creative persons tend to be nonconformists with the ability to pursue creative ideas in the teeth of societal pressures to leave things as others have found them.[11] Creativity may also be thought of in reference to a particular act. Jerome Bruner speaks of creativity as an act that produces "effective surprise." *Surprise*, in this context refers to the unexpected, which elicits wonder or astonishment.[12] Effective surprises have the quality of obviousness attached to them. For example, Archimedes discovered some of the basic laws of hydrostatics, particularly the principle named after him which explains buoyancy. According to Archimedes' principle, an object placed in a liquid loses an amount of weight equal to the weight of the fluid it replaces. *Of course*, we think, but only after Archimedes' creative thinking has revealed the principle.

Creativity as a Process

Creativity is also a process, one involving four periods: (1) the preparation period, or a time of intense preoccupation with a problem and with identifying the difficulty; (2) the incubation period, a time of unconscious work; (3) the illumination period, the stage in which one searches for a solution, makes guesses, or formulates a hypothesis about the deficiencies; and (4) the verification period, a time of testing and revising one's hypotheses and communicating the results to others.[13]

Creativity as a Product

Creativity can be seen as a product, or bringing something new into existence. One researcher believes that all definitions of creativity have one essential ingredient, namely, the capacity to make new and valuable

10 Bailin, 109.

11 Richard J. Penaskovic, "Toward a Definition of Creativity," 103. See Mihaly Csikszentmihalyi, *Creativity: Flow and the Psychology of Discovery and Invention* (N.Y.: Harper Collins Publishers, 1996) and Jerome D. Oremland, *The Origins and Psychodynamics of Creativity; A Psychoanalytic Perspective* (Madison, Conn.: International Universities Press, 1997).

12 Jerome S. Bruner, "The Conditions of Creativity," in *Contemporary Approaches to Creative Thinking*, eds. E. Gruber *et al* (New York: Atherton, 1963), 5.

13 Penaskovic, 104.

products.[14] Output, then, is an important criterion for creativity. To be creative is to produce creative results by the standards of the discipline. Da Vinci, Michelangelo, Picasso, and Bach were all creative in this sense.

Finally, creativity may be applied to the human person as such. Abraham Maslow saw an overlap between creativity and the self-actualizing, fully human person. We have the widest scope for creative thinking in our own lives. They are a subject in which each of us is steeped, and one in which we can access information available to no one else. We act creatively all the time in finding ways to overcome the barriers that prevent us from reaching our goals.[15]

Creativity is, ultimately, the ability to transcend the confines of convention. Creativity means connecting the familiar with the unfamiliar or novel in an unexpected and stimulating way. In the classroom the familiar refers to what the student knows about the current topic under discussion. The unfamiliar is what the faculty member is attempting to teach. Faculty can demonstrate creative teaching by bringing about a marriage between what students already know and the course content.[16] I see output as the ultimate criterion of creativity. The creative person turns out original research according to the criteria of the domain in question. In twentieth-century religious thought, for example, Karl Barth, Rudolf Bultmann, Paul Tillich, Pierre Teilhard de Chardin, and Reinhold Niebuhr are thought to be creative thinkers because of the originality and extent of their work.

Creative thinking depends on intrinsic as opposed to extrinsic motivation. Creative individuals are in the driver's seat in terms of what they research and how. They see the task as worthwhile in itself and derive intellectual joy from doing it. One must have considerable expertise in the domain in question in order to produce work that is creative. One reason so little creative work is done in religious studies has to do with conventional schooling. Knowledge is presented to students as a given as opposed to being a creative effort to accomplish something. Many of the assignments we give students allow insufficient elbow room for them to be creative.

Critical and Creative Thinking

Common wisdom sees critical thinking and creative thinking as polar opposites. Critical thinking is *evaluative* whereas creative thinking is *gen-*

[14] Margaret Gilchrist, *The Psychology of Creativity* (Carlton, Victoria: Melbourne University, 1973), 99.

[15] Mary Henle, "The Birth and Death of Ideas," in *Contemporary Approaches to Creative Thinking*, eds. Howard E. Gruber et al. (New York: Atherton, 1962), 48. See Abraham Maslow, *The Farther Reaches of Human Nature* (New York: Viking, 1971), 69.

[16] Thomas A. Angelo and K. Patricia Cross, *Classroom Assessment Techniques: A Handbook for College Teachers*, Second Edition, (San Francisco: Jossey-Bass Publishers, 1993), 181.

erative. This section emphasizes the complementary nature of critical and creative thinking. In fact, it is impossible to delineate a hard and fast line between critical and creative thinking because all good thinking involves both evaluation and the production of something new. Critical thinkers must come up with ways to test their assertions; creative thinkers must assess the validity and usefulness of their new ideas. The difference between the two is one of degree and emphasis, not one of kind.

Critical and creative thinking should be taught together in the context of religious studies. Students develop critical thinking skills when they ask questions, define terms, or analyze a text or film critically. They develop their creative talents when they plan papers or projects and solve unstructured problems. Students think both critically and creatively when they reflect on diverse viewpoints and reconstruct them critically and imaginatively.[17]

Faculty can foster critical and creative thinking in religious studies by having students engage in the following:

1. Organize panel discussions or debates on controversial subjects. In a course on religious pluralism, I had students defend the viewpoints of an inclusivist, an exclusivist, and a religious pluralist. Each panel member had five minutes for an oral presentation, followed by an exchange of views on religious pluralism among the panel and then among the class members.
2. Have students write an editorial in which they express their views on a specific issue. I give students three bonus points for doing this exercise. I also give them guidelines on writing the letter: address a specific issue, write succinctly, use other letters to the editor as a guide, and give a complete address and phone number.
3. Have students analyze journal/newspaper articles to find instances of bias. To get them started, ask such questions as the following: Does the author present his or her subject in a favorable or unfavorable way? Are any important facts omitted or glossed over? Is the author's tone friendly or hostile?
4. Invite speakers with controversial views to give guest lectures in your class. In a course on theological ethics, for example, I have a speaker from Planned Parenthood and one from a right-to-life organization speak to my class (not on the same day, though).
5. For courses with a strong, historical emphasis, such as the History of Christianity, I have asked students to role-play historical incidents in which protagonists held divergent views: Luther's debate with John Eck, for instance, works well. I have also had students

---

[17] Robert J. Marzano *et al*, eds., *Dimensions of Thinking: A Framework for Curriculum and Instruction* (Alexandria, VA: Association for Supervision and Curriculum Development, 1988), 28.

dress up as a historical figure, Buddha, for example, and tell the figure's life story in a highly personal way. They must stay "in character" through questions.

6. Four weeks into a course ask students this question: How can this course better meet your needs? Have students write out their comments in class. You may be surprised what students say. Many times students will come up with some super ideas that are easy to implement. This exercise also tells students that their ideas are worthwhile and that you, the faculty member, are open to their suggestions. A spin-off of this question is to ask how the course is relevant to students' personal lives.

Practical Applications

The following techniques help students create and faculty members assess synthetic and creative thinking. Concept maps and annotated portfolios, in particular, help students make their knowledge structures explicit. In this way both students and faculty can better understand them. I have drawn heavily on the work of Thomas A. Angelo and K. Patricia Cross in their book, *Classroom Assessment Techniques*, which I have modified and made relevant to the academic study of religion.[18]

Word Journals

Word journals require students to sum up a brief text or video in one word and provide a one- or two-page rationale for choosing that particular word. The word-journal assignment allows the instructor to assess students' creativity in summing up what they have read, and it helps develop students' ability to think for themselves and to think holistically— that is, to see the whole as well as the parts. It also indicates students' ability to synthesize and integrate ideas. The word journal also encourages active learning through reading and thus supports the objectives outlined in chapter five of this book.

The word journal is particularly well-suited to courses that emphasize primary texts as opposed to textbooks. Use it to assess the reading of scripture, short articles, case histories, and short essays. Two words of caution about using the word journal, however: (1) it is a useful technique only if reading and summarizing skills are an important part of your course since it takes time to prepare, analyze, and discuss; (2) the word journal should not be employed when there exists only one way to summarize the material. It works best when students have the liberty to offer their own interpretations.

[18] Angelo and Cross, 188–192.

I used the word journal in a seminar course on critical thinking and the academic study of religion. Two students in the seminar summarized the first chapter of the text in one word and then wrote two paragraphs stating why they chose that particular word. They used the summaries to lead a discussion on the key concepts found in the chapter. The following week two other students followed the same procedure. This continued for the rest of the quarter until each student had summarized two chapters of the text. For me this solved the problem of getting students to read the text carefully. I knew with certainty that for each class meeting at least two students had closely read the assignment.

Here are some hints for turning the responses to the word journal into useful information:

1. Write your own list of summary words for the particular chapter, jotting down some analyses/arguments that you find plausible in defense of the word choices students will make.
2. Have students develop criteria for evaluating the word journals; that is, help students come up with a list of the qualities that mark a good response. Students should scrutinize not only the choice of words but the reasons for their choices.
3. Break the class into dyads to analyze the pluses and minuses of each other's word journals. It cannot be stressed enough that unless students discuss and compare their responses, they will derive little benefit from this exercise.[19]

Approximate Analogies

Approximate analogies, so called because they do not have to meet the rigorous requirement of formal logic or mathematics, give students guided practice in making connections. Students complete the second half of an analogy such as A is to B as X is to Y, for which the instructor has supplied the first half (A is to B). This exercise permits faculty to discover whether students understand the relationship between the two terms found in the first half of the analogy, and they develop in students an openness to novel ideas, the capacity to think for themselves, and the ability to think creatively. This simple technique can be used in any course in religious studies with classes ranging in size from 1 to 250 students.

To create approximate analogies pick a key relationship between two concepts or terms that you want your students to know. Use the two related concepts/facts as the A and B parts in the format "A:B = X:Y." Then generate a number of approximate completions, the X: Y part. Here are some examples:

[19] Ibid, 191.

Complete the following by filling in the correct word in the blank.

1. The <u> sacred </u> is to the profane as transcendence is to immanence.
2. Pure or philosophical ethics : theological ethics as natural theology: <u>revelation</u> .
3. Judaism : Islam as <u> Torah </u> : shariah.
4. Karl Barth : <u> neo-orthodoxy </u> as Gustavo Gutierriez : liberation theology.
5. Descartes : modern philosophy as <u> Kant </u> : the Enlightenment.

You may modify the above exercise in several ways. Ask students to give a reason for their responses and make this worth one extra point. Or have students explain the type of relationship found in the approximate analogy and make this worth one point more. Finally, have students generate their own approximate analogies based on the material covered in the class so far.

Many of my students find this technique to be intellectually challenging. Approximate analogies allow students to connect new knowledge in religious studies to prior knowledge. These types of connections encourage meaningful and lasting learning. Approximate analogies are easier for students who have extensive vocabularies and broad reading experience, and some students may have trouble with them. In that case, provide plenty of examples so that they understand what you want them to do.[20]

Concept Maps
Concept maps are similar to brainstorming, except here the connections are made visually rather than verbally. Concept maps may be understood as a schematic device for representing a set of concept meanings embedded in a framework of propositions. More simply, a concept map is two concepts connected by a linking word to form a proposition, for instance, the statement that "the sun is a star."[21]

Concept maps are, then, a kind of visual reinforcement in which the main idea or subject is written down in the center of the paper and circled. Subordinate points are also jotted down and circled. Then connecting lines are drawn from each point to the main idea and to each other, if appropriate. Other relevant ideas are jotted down until a graphic representation of the text is made.

---

20 Ibid., 195.
21 Ibid, 197. See Ruth Shagoury Hubbard, "Reclaiming the Power of Visual Thinking with Adult Learners," in *New Entries: Learning by Writing and Drawing*, Ruth Shagoury Hubbard and Karen Ernst, eds. (Portsmouth, N.H.: Heinemann, 1996), 128–140.

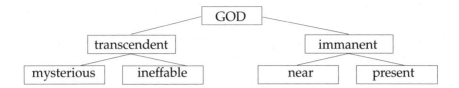

Concept maps aid faculty in figuring out the match between their conceptual map (which in this book is a "map" used by faculty in religious studies) and students' perception of relevant conceptual relations. Concept maps are diagrams or drawings that illustrate the connections that a student makes between prior knowledge and the concept the teacher focuses on. Just as a regular map provides a visual guide to a particular area, a concept map points out some of the paths we take to connect meaning among concepts.

Ideally, concept maps ought to be hierarchical, i.e., they should go from the more general concepts at the top of the map to more specific, less inclusive concepts at the bottom. Students need time to make up good concept maps. They also need practice in creating them. But concept maps can serve at least two important functions: (1) they can be tools for negotiating meaning, in the sense that meanings can be discussed, exchanged, and agreed upon by two or more students working in a small group; and (2) they are remarkably effective for showing misconceptions.

Use concept maps as a way of introducing a new concept in religious studies. You will discover what prior knowledge structures students bring to the class and uncover misconceptions that may later cause difficulties. Specific suggestions for using concept maps include the following:

1. Begin with a concept that is central to your course. A course on women in religion might use the term *feminism* as a jumping-off point. Or a course on the philosophy of religion might commence with putting the word *God* at the center of the paper and adding related concepts.
2. Give students a model to follow. At the beginning of a course or before starting a new topic, I like to have an idea of what my students know or do not know about a topic. Concept maps are a good way of assessing what my students know about a new topic. How does one begin? Select a pivotal concept from the new topic to be studied and ask students to build a concept map that indicates all the concepts/relationships they can make to this key concept. A glance at forty or fifty concept maps gives me a good indication about students' knowledge about a key concept. One can also spot

misconceptions or faulty linkages by looking at a student's concept map.

In the History of Christianity course I asked students to make a concept map of the term *dogma*. This is what some of them came up with.

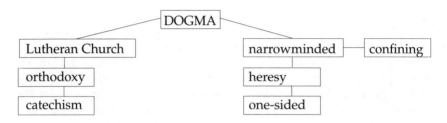

What is wrong with this concept map? Lutherans would use the term *doctrine* rather than *dogma*, which is a term Roman Catholics prefer. One way to assess concept differentiation is to select a dozen concepts and have students build a concept map using these concepts.

3. Have students brainstorm using a concept such as "faith," "theology," or "Islam" and use the solar system, a geographical map, or a wheel whose hub is the concept as a model. In a section of a course on Christian ethics I used the following concept map as a model for ethical method:

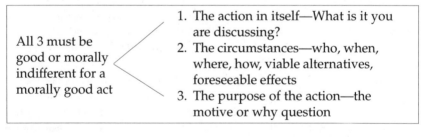

4. Have students figure out the relationships between various concepts and write them down on the lines connecting the concepts.
5. Make up a concept map yourself so you know first hand the difficulties involved in drawing one. Use your map to make sure students understand the process.

Various spin-offs are possible with the concept map. Have students write an explanatory essay on the basis of their maps. Or have students buy large-format graph paper for their concept maps and calculate the distance between the focus concept and related concepts. Assign a concept map in lieu of an essay question on a midterm or final examination.

Grading a concept map can be difficult. I use my own concept map as a touchstone to compare the students' maps. Students will come up with some unusual relationships that may surprise you, but consider the content of the map and the type of relations found among concepts.[22]

Invented Dialogues
Invented dialogues offer a unique way to develop students' creativity and ability to synthesize information. They help develop students' historical perspective and practice their skills in drawing intelligent inferences from observations. Have students make up invented dialogues by combining real quotes from primary sources or created quotes that fit the context and the character of the speakers. A good example of an invented dialogue is the conversation between Jesus and the Buddha that Paul Knitter made up in his book *Faith , Religion and Theology*.[23]

Use invented dialogues in courses on Hebrew scriptures, the New Testament, the history of Christianity, religion in America, and twentieth-century religious thought. Suggest the issues, person, and topics to be covered in order to give the dialogues focus. In a course on the Hebrew scriptures, for example, have students make up a dialogue between God and Moses at the top of Mt. Sinai. Or in a course on the history of Christianity have them imagine a conversation between Luther and Erasmus on free will or one between Anabaptists and Roman Catholics on infant baptism or one between Muslims and Hindus on the nature of God.

The following are suggestions for maximizing the usefulness of invented dialogues:

1. Choose a person, theory, or issue that is central to your course and that lends itself to the dialogue format. In an introduction to religion course have students create a dialogue on the origin of religion according to Frazer, Durkheim, and Freud.
2. Give students specific directions on the format of the dialogue, suggesting possible topics, time, and length, and list your criteria for a first-rate dialogue. Tell your students that they are to invent a natural, persuasive, original dialogue based on quotes from the characters.
3. Write a dialogue yourself and share your experience with students.
4. Do not squelch your students' creativity by giving them too many guidelines.
5. Remember that some students may need their hand held as they work through this exercise. For the first dialogue, you might have students work in dyads. Allow students to polish their dialogues

[22] Ibid., 201.
[23] Brennan Hill, William Madges and Paul Knitter, *Faith, Religion and Theology: A Contemporary Introduction* (Mystic, CT: Twenty-Third Publications, 1990), 221–247.

after you have looked them over and made suggestions. Have students turn the dialogues into an essay or ask for volunteers to act out their dialogue or present it on videotape for the entire class. Invented dialogues provide more room for creative thinking than book reviews and traditional term papers.[24]

As you grade dialogues ask how well students have synthesized the material. How original or creative are the dialogues? How well are the dialogues written?

Annotated Portfolios

Annotated portfolios highlight the creative work of students along with the students' own commentary on that work as it relates to a particular course. They permit faculty to see how students make connections between their creative work and the course content, and faculty come to see how students can apply what they have learned and whether or not their creativity and self-assessment skills are developing.[25]

In many fields, particularly in the fine arts, portfolios are common practice. Graphic artists, photographers, architects, and painters show samples of their works to prospective employers, admission committees of graduate schools, and foundations. Continuing education programs of colleges and universities often allow returning adults to construct a portfolio of their work and life experience, supplemented by supporting documentation, to substitute for some college courses.

Instead of doing a term paper or book review, I offer students the opportunity to have their assignment grade based on the execution of a project. For instance, an architecture student made a scale model of a Shinto temple out of Popsicle sticks. An anthropology student made a model of an Egyptian pyramid. An artist painted several pictures with religious themes, and a student of the Japanese martial arts put on an outdoor demonstration of the use of wooden sticks in fighting. The latter was a martial arts teacher and had four of his students demonstrate for the entire class.

In order to elicit such a wide range of responses from students, I ask them to choose the topic on which to focus their portfolio. My only requirement is that it be closely related to the course outline. Allowing the annotated portfolio use in lieu of a regular traditional assignment gives students latitude in expressing their creativity by working in images and other media rather than in prose alone. Several students have, for example, made their own movies—and served popcorn. Annotated portfolios allow me to glimpse what students value.

24 Angelo and Cross, 207.
25 Ibid., 208.

Annotated portfolios must be well integrated into the course. Meet with the student or groups of students who want to use them to keep tabs on their work and to be an informal consultant.

The Use of Intuition in Religious Studies

Logical and rational thought uses words, and intuitive and emotional thought takes advantage of the insight available in images, sounds, and symbols. Intuitive thought gives us guidance and insight when our logical, linear thinking reaches its limit. Intuitive techniques make use of our right-brain capability to see the solution to a problem in a sudden leap of logic. Is our intuitive self synonymous with the subconscious? Probably not. Our subconscious contains memories and related thoughts and emotions that may directly affect our daily life. Our intuitive self makes its presence known when our subconscious has been quieted. In order to access our intuitive self we need to gently set aside our traditional habits, emotions, and beliefs and nurture calmness.

The literature on stress management contains many methods for relaxation. This is one I have used effectively with my students.

> Imagine yourself on a quiet lake. The sun is out in full force and you are relaxing on a float and you are feeling completely relaxed. You have not a care in the world and you just love looking at the blue sky and picking up the sun's soothing rays. A feeling of heaviness is coming over your right fingertips, your right hand, your wrist, and your whole right arm. At the same time you are feeling completely and fully relaxed. This feeling of heaviness is now present in your right foot, your toes, and your entire right leg. Then this feeling of heaviness is spreading to your left side from your fingertips, your left hand, and your left arm. Pretty soon this feeling of heaviness is present throughout your body and you are feeling completely relaxed. Now there is one part of your body that is feeling more relaxed than any other part. Identify this part of your body and feel this relaxation spreading to the rest of your body.

This exercise is very powerful and works well with students.

Intuitive Techniques

I have used the following techniques in my religious studies courses: symbols and maps, imagery, brainstorming, analogy, dreams, drawing, and meditation. A symbol may be defined as something that stands for, or points to, something else.[26] Much of human behavior involves a process of symbolizing through which words, gestures, and objects stand for something other than themselves. In the sacrament of the Eucharist the consecrated bread and wine symbolize the presence of Christ.

---

[26] Roger Schmidt, *Exploring Religion* (Belmont, CA: Wadsworth, Inc., 1980), 84.

While the Torii, the Gateway to the shrine, represents Shintoism, a Jewish star represents Judaism. Accepted symbols make it possible for us to share our experiences because people generally agree on what the symbols represent. The rings in a marriage ceremony, for instance, stand for fidelity and commitment.

To teach students about symbols, ask them to draw a picture of two or three symbols that have special meaning for them. Then have them write out the feelings these symbols represent. The meaning of these symbols may or may not be shared by other people. Teach about symbols in general before discussing religious symbols. As a practical exercise, have students choose an item—hair, uniform, music, regional accent, earrings, cigarette brand—and explain how it can serve as a symbol:

Symbol	What the Symbol Stands For
1. Nuptial ring	1. Marriage
2. U.S. flag	2. Patriotism
3. A dozen roses	3. Love

Next, have students identify two to three symbols of a particular kind and describe what they represent:

Status Symbols	What the Symbol Represents
1. Lexus	1. Money/success
2. Gold neck chain	2. Athleticism
3. Rolex watch	3. Affluence

Religious Symbols	What the Symbol Represents
1. Jewish star	1. Israel, Judaism
2. Torii	2. Shintoism
3. Yin-Yang	3. Confucianism

Maps and Symbols

Symbols are usually clustered together in groups. In fact, maps are groups of symbols organized in a special way. What makes a map meaningful is the way various symbols are joined to make a *Gestalt*, or whole that is meaningful. Have students make a map from their classroom on campus to their place of residence. Then ask them to translate this visual map into a verbal map. This process of creating and organizing symbols in order to make sense of the world is essential to our thought processes.

Each of us constructs a mental blueprint of who we are. No one comes into the world knowing who he or she is or shall be. Psychologists call this map our "self-concept." To tap into students' blueprints, have them write down ten words to describe themselves. Then ask them to create a map that expresses certain aspects of themselves using the ten words as points of reference. The map we construct may be accurate or inaccurate. We have a realistic understanding of ourselves if our map is reasonably accurate. When our map is inaccurate, we are operating with an unrealistic or distorted view of ourselves.

This is the map I drew of myself:

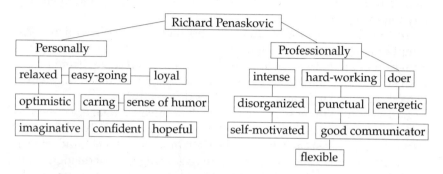

Require students to construct a map of themselves during the first week of class and share it in their cooperative learning group. This helps build solidarity within the group. I also tell students to determine their own level of participation or non-participation in this exercise. That is, they are not required to share their map with the group but are encouraged to do so.

A Map of Others

We unconsciously construct maps to understand other people in our lives. We do this because human beings display a certain organizational pattern. Our beliefs about others can be regarded as a map of their personality. We will be able to make sense of the things others are doing in the present, understand how they have acted in the past, and to some extent predict how they will act in the future if our map of them is accurate. Have students select a partner from their group whom they do not know very well. Have them 1) describe the person in ten words; 2) create a map of him or her; 3) interview the person and try to find out information about him or her from other members in the group. What are the person's goals in life, values, and beliefs?; 4) construct a revised map of this person and compare it with the one you initially formed. Compare and contrast the two maps.[27]

[27] Joseph D. Novak and D. Bob Gowin, *Learning How to Learn.* (Cambridge, England: C U P, 1987), 15–54. See Angelo and Cross, 197–202.

Imagery and the Imagination

Our culture lacks neither intelligence nor expertise in technology. However, we do lack the ability to imagine. And this lack may bring us to our knees. The ability to imagine may also be the most difficult ability to teach because we know precious little about it and it is such a supremely personal faculty. Imagination requires exercise, however, or it will grow remote from our everyday lives and leave us emotionally and intellectually impoverished.

Try this exercise first by yourself and then with your students. Attempt to imagine yourself. Beware of false images. We all carry around images that are not our own, many that we have received from others both close and distant from us. Now try to imagine yourself differently. What is involved in imagining ourselves differently?

Reflect with students on what imagery means. Imagery refers to mental images collectively, particularly those produced by the imagination. Psychologists believe that the right brain uses images rather than words to communicate. One can use images to engage in a dialogue with one's intuition and then abstract the qualities of the images into words. Begin the dialogue by asking a series of questions and then looking inside one's mind for whatever images emerge.[28]

The more one can create an experience using clear multisensory images, the more powerfully one's intuition can communicate. I advise students to talk to the images they receive and listen to what they say. When a threatening or frightening image appears ask for the next "deeper" image. A calmer image will emerge, one that can be worked with in a satisfactory way. The more one works with one's images, the more comfortable and relaxed one becomes in using them. As we befriend our intuition, we are then able to accept the truth it reveals to us.

How to Begin

I have used several guided imagery techniques in my courses. In the beginning some students will be uncomfortable with the process. To counteract this one should completely explain the imagery process and the benefits of using it before any imagery sessions are commenced. I tell my students that an imagery process is as normal as daydreaming.

---

[28] See Mary Ann Smorra, "Using Mnemonics and Visual Imagery to Facilitate Critical Thinking," in *Critical Thinking: Implications for Teaching and Teachers. Proceedings of the 1991 Conference.* eds. Wendy Oxman et al. (Upper Montclair, NJ: The Institute for Critical Thinking, 1992), 288–292. Metaphor is a way of representing experience, a form of representation that lies at the heart of literary cognition. On the application of metaphorical thinking to literary character analysis, see Gregory Rubano and Philip M. Anderson, "Metaphorical Portraits of Literary Characters," in *Teaching Critical Thinking: Reports from Across the Curriculum* John H. Clarke and Arthur W. Biddle, eds. (Englewood Cliffs, N.J.: Prentice Hall, 1993), 146–155.

For those who are reluctant to try the imagery experience, have them close their eyes and simply relax during the session.

I introduce students to imagery by asking them to close their eyes and count the rooms in the house they lived in as a child. I request that they go through each room and tell me what they notice. Students are often amazed by how many things they see such as a fire in the fireplace, tinsel on the Christmas tree, or dust on the dresser drawers. After this non-threatening introduction to mental imagery, the students are receptive to further exercises.

Guided Imagery

Undergraduates can really relate to guided imagery exercises.[29] I may turn down the lights in the classroom when I do the following exercise. I ask students to close their eyes and to relax as completely as they can. They are then to imagine themselves in a quiet forest with lush foliage and vegetation. As they are walking in the forest, they suddenly come upon a cleared out area of about 50 feet wide. There in the center of the clearing, they see a huge black chest with words in white that read "The Secret of Creation."

They are unsure whether to open the chest or not. Finally, they decide to do so and when they do, they see several items inside. What do they see inside the chest? Open your eyes and write down what you see inside the Secret of Creation chest. I ask students to write a page of what they see. They are then broken into groups of four to share their responses. One student saw Oral Roberts inside, smiling knowingly. Another student peered inside and saw God as First Cause.

Here is another guided imagery exercise that works well with students. Imagine yourself at a quiet lake. The water is very gentle with no breeze. You are on a float feeling perfectly relaxed. You are getting hot from the direct rays of the sun and decide to plunge under water. To your amazement you find that you can breathe underwater. You decide to explore the bottom of the lake and find yourself walking fifty feet below the surface. You see various fish swim by, some small, some quite large. Out of the blue you see a luminescent fish about six feet long. It swims near you. At first you are frightened, but as the fish swims by it speaks to you and says, "Relax, I won't harm you. I am all-knowing. Ask me anything." What question do you ask the all-knowing fish and what answer does the fish give to your question? Students write a 200-word essay on this. Then they share their questions and answers in small groups before processing them in the larger group.

[29] See Walter J. Wheatley, et al, "Guided Imagery in the Management Class," in *Teaching Critical Thinking: Reports from Across the Curriculum* pp.221–230.

Centering Prayer

For those who teach a course on spirituality, a session on centering prayer may fit well into one of your classes. Centering prayer arises from ancient traditions, both Eastern and Western. Centering prayer means to gently put aside all thoughts and images so that we transcend the senses and the rational mind in hopes of finding God or the transcendent/ sacred at the center of our being.

Creating an Inner Space

Have students close their eyes and imagine a square made out of any material. Inside the square picture a circle. Inside the circle put a triangle. Move toward the triangle. It will grow larger as one approaches it. The circle becomes a very long tunnel. Move into the tunnel and continue on toward the triangle. It will grow larger as you approach it. The circle becomes a very long tunnel. Move into the tunnel and continue on toward the triangle. Pass through the center of the triangle and rest there. This is a very powerful exercise. Take your time when having students create an inner space for centering prayer.

Three Rules

Remember that centering prayer does not replace other types of prayer. Rather, it puts them into a new and fuller perspective. One attains the experience of God by going to one's center and passing through it into the center of God or the sacred. These are the three rules for centering prayer:

1. At the start, take two minutes to quiet down. Move in faith to God or the sacred dwelling in one's heart.
2. After resting a while in the center, choose a simple word to express your response and let it repeat itself within.
3. If distractions arise, gently return to God's presence using the prayer word. Take several minutes to exit the exercise, mentally saying the Lord's prayer or slowly counting down from ten to one.

Summary

This chapter commenced with a brief look at the barriers to teaching creatively and a discussion of the nature of creativity. It stresses the complementary nature of critical and creative thinking. One cannot delineate a hard and fast boundary between critical and creative thinking because good thinking involves both evaluation and the production of something new.

Several techniques were looked at to help students create and faculty members assess synthetic and creative thinking: word journals, approximate analogies, concept maps, invented dialogues, annotated portfolios, intuitive techniques, maps and symbols, guided imagery, and centering prayer. The next chapter looks at assessment and offers faculty some practical strategies for the assessment of critical thinking.

7

The Assessment of Critical Thinking

*"Effective teaching involves the clear statement of what students
are supposed to learn, an atmosphere that is conducive to learning,
engaging and interesting activities that provide opportunities to
learn, and dependable measures of student outcomes."*

Thomas M. Haladyna

The term assessment means many things. It applies to a wide range of
approaches used to measure educational effectiveness.[1] Assessment has
as its major goal the improvement of the teaching/learning process. The
assessment movement travels down two different but related roads. The
first road is called program evaluation. In program evaluation patterns
of student performance are scrutinized, often with standardized tests
developed outside of the institution. Institutions use the results of assessment to see how groups of students are doing and to determine the
need for overall instructional improvement.

The other road assessment takes may be called student evaluation.
Whereas program evaluation has assessment on the institutional level as
its primary concern, student evaluation focuses on individual student
learning. Student evaluation answers the question: What are *my* students
learning in *my* class as a result of *my* instruction?[2] The consequences of
student performance are listed in terms of the student's future improve-

---

[1] Thomas A. Angelo and K. Patricia Cross, *Classroom Assessment Techniques; A Handbook
for College Teachers*, Second Edition, (San Francisco: Jossey-Bass Publishers, 1993), 7.
See Barbara Gross Davis *Tools for Teaching* (San Francisco: Jossey-Bass Publishers, 1993),
239–298 for a discussion for testing and grading. See Mary Kay Crouch and Sheryl I.
Fontaine, "Student Portfolios as an Assessment Tool," in *Changing College Classrooms*, ed.
Halpern and Associates (San Francisco: Jossey-Bass, 1994), 306–328; Thomas M. Haladyna,
Developing and Validating Multiple-Choice Tests Items (Hillsdale, N.J.: Lawrence Erlbaum As-
sociates, Publishers, 1994); Charles H. Hargis, *Curriculum Based Assessment: A Primer*,
Second Edition (Springfield, Illinois: Charles C. Thomas, Publisher, 1995); and Robert Roth-
man, *Measuring Up: Standards, Assessment and School Reform* (San Francisco: Jossey-Bass
Publishers, 1995).

[2] Susan G. Nunmedal, "How Classroom Assessment Can Improve Teaching And Learning," *Changing College Classrooms*, 292.

ment. Although such assessment focuses on the student, faculty can also determine the kinds of institutional changes needed to improve student performance on future assessments.[3]

This chapter looks at assessment solely in terms of student evaluation. After defining what we means by assessment, several features of the assessment process are noted. We argue that assessment is at the heart of the learning process. Instructors in religious studies need to fit assessment techniques to their specific classes, their individual teaching goals, and their particular students. The advice given in this chapter may be summed up in the phrase "Adapt, rather than adopt."

Formative vs. Summative Evaluations

Student evaluations may be either formal (summative) or informal (formative). Faculty use methods such as tests, examinations, or quizzes to evaluate student learning formally. They may also use homework, term papers, journals, or book reviews to formally evaluate students. Summative evaluations are then used to assign grades and to determine individual student achievement.

Informal or formative evaluations are used primarily to improve learning and inform teaching.[4] Most faculty have a repertoire of techniques to evaluate classroom learning informally. These include such items as observing body language, facial expressions, attending carefully to student comments and questions, and posing such questions as "Are you with me in my explanation of hermeneutics?" Informal or formative evaluations make it possible for faculty to slow down or repeat an explanation in response to confusion, questions, or misunderstandings or move on to a new topic because students are *with* the instructor.

The Process of Classroom Assessment

Many faculty gather information about their students automatically and as a matter of course. Starting on the first day of class we attempt to get a handle on our students and their level of sophistication in regard to their knowledge of religion. Impressions are formed, but, for the most part, this functions as an informal, implicit, even unconscious process. In my experience faculty rarely make their impressions explicit in order to check their on-line assessments against the students' own impression or abilities to perform. We make assumptions about our students' learning, and, as a rule, these assumptions go untested.

---

3 Lucy Cromwell, "Assessing Critical Thinking," *Critical Thinking: Educational Imperative.* New Directions for Community Colleges No. 77: (Spring, 1992), 37–50.

4 Thomas A. Angelo and K. Patricia Cross, 5.

Identify Teaching Goals

Effective assessment commences with a description of one's teaching goals. Goals are both destinations we set out for as well as reference points that are used to measure our progress and to decide whether or not we are headed in the right direction. It is imperative that faculty identify and clarify what they are trying to teach. Otherwise, it is impossible to assess how well their students are learning. By starting with teaching goals, faculty can get a handle on what they believe is most important to teach and what they want students to learn.[5]

There are several advantages of starting with goals. First, it encourages faculty to do a self-assessment of their teaching aims. Second, it promotes good instructional practice by making sure that faculty are teaching what they are assessing and assessing what they are teaching. Third, beginning with goals creates the basis for a shared vocabulary, which faculty in a department of Religious Studies can use in discussing their classroom assessment projects

There is a downside to beginning with goals. Some faculty may be threatened by identifying and clarifying goals. In my experience in teaching over the past twenty years, instructional goals are rarely discussed explicitly by college faculty. Moreover, there exists a wide chasm between stating an instructional goal, such as "I want my students to learn to think critically," and knowing how to assess that goal in a specific course.

Instead of beginning with goals, one may begin assessment with a simple question. For some faculty, starting with questions is more immediately familiar than a goal-based approach. For those faculty in religious studies who are in charge of internship programs, they may begin their assessment by asking a simple question like "What goals do my students have for the first day of their internship?"[6]

If professors are unclear about what they want to assess and why, then the feedback they receive from classroom assessment cannot serve its intended purpose. One must not begin from scratch in formulating teaching and learning goals. One may consult the Teacher Goals Inventory and Self-Scoreable Worksheet developed by Thomas A. Angelo and K. Patricia Cross. It is a self-assessment of instructional goals that aids faculty in becoming more aware of what they hope to accomplish in individual courses. One may use the work of Angelo and Cross to create one's own discipline-specific feedback devices.[7]

---

5 Ibid., 8. See William A. Mehrens and Irvin J. Lehmann, *Measurement And Evaluation In Education And Psychology* Fourth Edition, (Fort Worth: Holt, Rinehart and Winston, Inc., 1991), 44.

6 Ibid., 45.

7 Ibid., 393–397. For the best book on writing test items, see Thomas M. Haladyna, *Writing Test Items to Evaluate Higher Order Thinking* (Boston: Allyn and Bacon, 1997), 61–220.

One may also bring students into the assessment process by asking them to list their teaching and learning goals for a specific course. I have been doing this for over a decade now with excellent results.On the first day of class I ask students to write down five goals for the course, apart from getting an "A".

I suggest that instructors try out a couple of classroom assessment techniques (CAT) if they are unfamiliar with classroom assessment. It will require only five to ten minutes of in-class time and less than an hour of time out of class. After doing a couple of assessments, faculty can determine whether this approach is worth pursuing.

The following streamlined, three-step process maximizes the likelihood of success for those attempting to do classroom assessment for the first time.

Step 1: Planning.   Do your first assessment on a course that you are thoroughly familiar with and in which students are doing well. After choosing a focus class, reserve a few minutes for the assessment. Select a CAT that is adaptable to many situations and simple, such as the minute paper, the muddiest point, the one-sentence summary, directed paraphrasing, or application cards. The minute paper asks students two question: (1) What was the most important thing you learned today? and (2) What further questions do you have as a result of today's class? The muddiest point technique is a version of the minute paper and deals with the question: What was the muddiest point in today's session?[8]

The one-sentence summary asks students to summarize a large amount of information on a given topic in a single sentence. One may ask students to sum up a historical event (such as the Reformation in Germany), the plot of a short story, or a chapter in the book.[9] One may use a chart like the following to help students do the summary.

Who?	Martin Luther
Does what?	Breaks with the Catholic Church
To what or whom?	Over the question of indulgences
When?	In 1517
Where?	In Wittenberg
How?	By nailing the 95 Theses to the door of the cathedral
Why?	In order to call attention to the abuses associated with indulgences

[8] Ibid., 154–158. See Susan G. Nunmedal, 293.
[9] Ibid., 183–187.

In sentence form: Martin Luther broke with the Roman Catholic Church in 1517 by nailing the 95 Theses to the door of the cathedral in Wittenberg in order to call attention to the abuses associated with indulgences.

Directed paraphrasing asks students to paraphrase a concept or procedure in two to three sentences for a specific audience. Directed paraphrasing assesses the ability of students to apply declarative knowledge to a new context. Because the paraphrase is aimed at a particular audience for a specific reason, the task of paraphrasing is more useful than simple paraphrasing. In a course on Eastern religions, for example, one may ask students to paraphrase their understanding of *satori* in terms their grandmothers could understand.[10]

Step 2: Implementing.   After choosing a focus course and a simple CAT to use in it, tell students you will be assessing their learning not to grade them, but to help them improve. I have had good success doing this by asking for anonymous responses. At the outset tell students how much time they will have to do the assessment exercise.

In analyzing the feedback from the muddiest point technique, notice how many times the same "muddy point" comes up. Student responses to the one-sentence summary or directed paraphrasing can be sorted easily into three piles: on-target responses, somewhat correct responses, or off-target/incorrect responses. The number of responses in each pile can then be counted, along with the approximate percentage of the total class each represents.[11]

Step 3: Responding.   Inform students about CAT results. Such feedback to students motivates them to become actively involved in the class and to improve their learning. For example, I ask for a course evaluation after one month of class.

I ask students to anonymously answer these questions: How are you doing in this class? How can the class be improved? Is it meeting your needs? If you were teaching this course, would you do anything differently? I then put students' comments into three columns: positive, negative and suggestions for improvement. I make a copy of this feedback for each student in class. Together, we discuss the results and talk

---

10 Ibid., 232–235. For some hints on helping students develop the difficult skill of achieving the critical distance needed to make accurate evaluations of their own work, see Eric H. Hobson, "Encouraging Self-Assessment: Writing as Active Learning," in *Using Active learning in College Classes: A Range of Options for Faculty*, Tracy E. Sutherland and Charles C. Bonwell, eds. (San Francisco: Jossey-Bass Publishers, 1996), 45–58.

11 Ibid., 30.

about improving the course. Most of the time I find confirmation of the teaching methods I use. Occasionally, I have to modify my approach to the course. Students may want a guest speaker or some movie dealing with the course content. Because their responses are anonymous, students feel free to comment on every aspect of the course. They once told me that I should wear more conservative ties!

Here are four suggestions to increase success in classroom assessment:

1. *Only use those classroom assessment techniques that appeal to you.* I feel that individual faculty members in Religious Studies are the best authorities on the improvement of teaching and learning in their classrooms. One instructor's favorite assessment technique may be another professor's poison.
2. *Begin in a small way.* Classroom assessment should not become a self-inflicted burden. Try one or two of these techniques in a semester rather than testing all of them in one semester or quarter. Your confidence and skill in the use of classroom assessment will increase with experience.
3. *If possible, use the classroom assessment technique on yourself before trying it out with a class.* By doing this you will see, first hand, where problems are likely to occur, how long the exercise takes, and whether any changes are necessary.
4. *Tell students what you learn from their feedback.* Students are more likely to participate in a positive way when they see how useful classroom assessment can be.

Classroom Assessment Projects

I have found it helpful to experiment with classroom assessment techniques for a semester or two before moving to the next step, classroom assessment projects. Once I learned to use the former with confidence, I was then able to link assessment more directly to my instructional goals.

There are several ways of assessing skill in analysis and critical thinking. This section contains four techniques that can be used to assess the skills of students in analyzing problems. These critical-thinking and analytical skills are instances of procedural learning. They are concerned with the "how" rather than the "what." They are arranged in order of progressively making greater demands on students.

The defining features matrix helps students observe and respond to discriminating features. This technique assesses the skill of students in categorizing information according to a set of critical defining features. The defining features matrix serves a dual role: for students, it helps identify and explicate the critical distinctions between apparently similar concepts; for faculty, it allows them to see how well students can discriminate between similar concepts.[12]

There are several areas in Religious Studies where a defining features matrix may be used. One such use is to have students construct a defining features matrix to compare and contrast religious studies with theology.

Features	Religious Studies	Theology
Began this century	+	-
Uses faith and reason as its sources of knowledge	-	+
Takes place in the academy	+	-

In a course on Eastern religions, one may use a defining features matrix to see how well students understood the detailed differences among the three main Chinese religions: Taoism, Chinese Buddhism and Confucianism, after students had read chapters on each of these religions. Or in an introduction to Religious Studies course, I have used the defining features matrix to assess the ability of students to distinguish between the phenomenological and the deconstructionist approach to the study of religion.

The defining features matrix has several important advantages: it gives students a powerful tool that they can use to categorize data; this technique has high transfer value, i.e., it can be used in many problem areas in religious studies; it allows faculty to pinpoint areas of confusion; and it helps both students and faculty break down complex comparisons and contrasts into smaller, more manageable component parts.

The following list contains some helpful hints in working with the Defining Features Matrix:

1. Construct a matrix yourself to see the difficulties involved in making one up.
2. Focus the matrix on two to three important concepts that students find confusing.
3. List defining features that each concept clearly does/does not have. One may add a small number of shared features after drawing up that list.

12 Ibid., 164–167.

4. See that each cell in the matrix can be responded to with a "yes" or "no," plus or minus sign. Remove those features of the cell that cannot be marked thus.
5. Draw up a finished matrix and have students copy it from the blackboard.
6. Explain clearly the purpose of the matrix, the time limit for filling it out, plus the directions for doing so.

Here are some ideas for expanding the defining features matrix:

1. Give students a defining features matrix on a topic related to your course. They can then use this matrix as a blueprint for creating their own defining features matrix to define items related to another topic covered in the course.
2. One can modify the simple binary responses in the cell by categorizing the features as "always present," "often present," "rarely present," and "never present."
3. Ask students to write a few sentences explaining what the pattern of responses in their completed matrix means.

Pro and Con Grid

Another way to assess critical thinking and analysis is the pro and con grid.[13] This grid gives faculty an overview of students' analyses of the advantages or disadvantages of an issue of mutual concern. By reading students' lists of pros and cons faculty are given vital information on the depth and breadth of students' analyses. Students, in turn, are forced to weigh the value of competing claims and are made to go beyond their initial reactions.

The pro and con grid may be used in courses that raise questions of value, such as Theological Ethics, Death and Dying, the Current Religious Scene, Introduction to Religious Studies, and Special Topics in Religion. The pro and con grid is an ideal way to assess how well students can use their imaginations to think about more than one side of an issue. The issues that students raise are good indications of which arguments they find to be very persuasive or troubling. One may focus on these arguments in future class discussions.

These are some ideas for using the pro and con grid in your classes:

1. Focus on an issue or dilemma that is important in your course.
2. Write out a sentence for students that will elicit a thoughtful response in terms of pros and cons.

---

13 Ibid., 168–171.

3. Tell students how the pros and cons are to be expressed—either in sentences or in parallel lists of words/phrases.
4. In turning the data collected into useful information, make a grid yourself. In this way you can compare students' pros and cons against yours. In giving feedback to the class, ask yourself if the pros and cons are balanced. Also determine whether students have added points that are extraneous or omitted some that are important.

The following are some brief examples that may be used in Religious Studies:

1. Should mandatory celibacy be the rule for Roman Catholic priests? Have students list three or four advantages of a married clergy as opposed to an equal number of disadvantages from the perspective of the church as an organization.
2. Suppose you are the curator of Native American collections at a museum in a large metropolitan center. Several Native American tribes have asked that museums and universities return human remains and tribal religious objects taken from their lands by explorers and archaeologists. Have students write a five-minute report for the board of directors of the museum on the pros and cons of returning these remains and objects.
3. There are any number of issues that can be examined in a medical ethics course using the pro and con grid. For instance, have your students read several articles on euthanasia. Have them make up a pro and con grid to discuss the advantages/disadvantages of performing cardiac resuscitation on an elderly patient in end-state heart failure. I have found that on certain ethical issues such as abortion, my students are unable to do the pro and con grid well because they are totally unable to see the other side of the argument. Some students may be upset with you for only bringing up certain issues for discussion. In responding to student anger and resistance, it is important to give proper respect for various viewpoints.

There are several ways of modifying the pro and con grid in order to increase student learning. One may use the results of the assessment as the point of departure for a pro and con essay assignment or for a class debate. Another idea is to have students back up their pros and cons with extended arguments once they have completed the pro and con grid itself. One can also ask students to use their imagination in listing pros and cons on an issue from diametrically opposed viewpoints, such as teacher and student, husband and wife, employer and employee, creditor and consumer.

Another classroom assessment technique is called a content, form, and function outline or a what, how, and why outline. In this exercise students analyze the content (what), the form (how), and the function or purpose (why) of an essay, a film, a poem, or a newspaper story. Then they compose a short memo answering the "what, how, and why" questions in an outline format.

This exercise helps faculty understand how students analyze the message, how it is presented, and its purpose. Content, form and function outlines develop reading, writing, analytical study skills, strategies, and habits. They also enhance the ability of students to make informed ethical choices, allowing students to think for themselves.[14]

The following book review on the theology of Karl Barth serves as a model for students in writing their own book reviews. I have then made a content, form and function outline based on my review in order to provide students with a practical example.

DIE THEOLOGIE KARL BARTH: EINE EINFÜHRUNG

By Christopher Frey. Frankfurt am Main: Athenaeum, 1988. Pp. 304. Paper, DM 48.

Who was the greatest theologian in the twentieth century? Some theologians would say E. Troeltsch. Frey argues that Karl Barth was and gives a plethora of reasons for his choice. This study shows the relationship between Barth's life and his thought, takes up his posture vis-à-vis Kant and Schleiermacher, and analyzes the changes in Barth's commentary on *Romans* between the first and second editions. It provides an excellent synopsis of the *Church Dogmatics* and concludes by suggesting how Barth's theology can be made fruitful today. This clear exposition of Barth's thought will appeal both to the beginning student in theology and also to Barth specialists. The author's command of the secondary literature on Barth in German is commendable. Regrettably, the author omits the many fine studies on Barth that have been published in French and English during the past decade.

Richard Penaskovic,
Auburn University

14 Ibid., 172–176.

A Content, Form, and Function Outline

Content (What?)	Form (How?)	Function (Why?)
Barth's theology	Book Review	To help scholars decide whether to order this book
Relationship between Barth's life and thought	Expository prose	To help readers understand the relationship between Barth's thought and life
Barth's relationship to Kant and Schleiermacher	Expository prose	To provide new insight into Barth's use of Kant and Schleiermacher
Changes in 1st and 2nd editions of Barth's *Epistle to the Romans*	Expository prose	To show scholars the development in Barth's thought
Summary of Barth's *Church Dogmatics*	Expository prose	To give scholars an overview of an extremely long study
Critique of Frey's book	Expository prose	To point out to scholars some limitations in Frey's book

The following are some points to keep in mind as you work with the content, form, and function outlines:

1. Some students will have difficulty with this exercise, and many will not succeed the first time. Hence one may want to give students several outlines to do. Analysis can be difficult for undergraduates since many texts, especially visual ones, perform several functions in each component part. I recommend using a clear and easily analyzed text the first time around. Also, repeat this technique over a period of several days.
2. Before students do the exercise, run through a sample one that you have done.

3. The first time through this exercise you may give undergraduates an outline form to follow. Such an outline will help you read responses more quickly.
4. Have students do the assessment outside of class unless it is a brief message or text. In this way you will not use up a lot of class time since the content, form and function outline is a time-intensive technique.

One can have students use the form, function and content outline to analyze the Sunday sermon either in a church of their choice or on T.V. One may also have students compare a live sermon to one on T.V.. A common error students make in doing this exercise is this: rather than analyzing the religious purposes of a sermon, many students respond by agreeing/disagreeing with the content. Faculty may need to discuss in class the difference between analyzing the preacher's message as opposed to evaluating it.

The analytic memo is another technique that I have used to assess critical thinking. However, this technique works best for small classes or seminars. The analytic memo asks students to analyze a concrete problem/issue in one to two pages. This writing assignment gives faculty feedback on their students' analytic and writing skills. It not only develops students' problem-solving and analytic skills, but it also develops students' management and leadership skills.[15]

Analytic memos work well when used early in the semester. They help students prepare for later graded writing assignments. In using analytic memos find an issue rich enough to generate reflective analysis. Then provide students with some background information or make up some plausible information. To motivate students to work on their analytic memos, I offer two points of extra credit for successfully doing this exercise.

I have used analytic memos in my Current Religious Scene course, where one of the topics is "Love and Marriage." I invent a plausible story about two college students who are head over heels in love and want to get married. I ask the students to play the role of the minister who must decide whether or not to marry this couple. Students were told to address the pros and cons of early marriage.

Here are some hints for turning the data collected from these memos into useful information. In reading each memo limit yourself to three points: "content" or the quality and breadth of the information, "skill" with which the relevant methods were employed in the analysis, and "overall writing quality." Then devise a checklist for each of these three

15 Ibid., 177–180.

points as you read, writing down "Excellent," "Good," or "Needs Improvement."

One may adapt the analytic memo by adding these wrinkles. Break students into dyads and ask them to evaluate each other's memos, providing guidelines for this task. Or divide the class into "ministers" and "couples" or "policy makers" vs. "policy analysts." Have the ministers write a letter to the couple who want to get married, and have the couple write a letter to the minister explaining why they should get married.

The following section discusses the assessment of skill in application and performance. It is concerned with what cognitive psychologists call "conditional" or "procedural" knowledge. It deals with the "when" and "where" for applying what one has learned. This section is very important because the lasting skills and knowledge undergraduates gain are those they learn to apply. We briefly touched upon this topic in this chapter when we spoke about directed paraphrasing, which asks students to translate their knowledge into language a specific audience will comprehend.

Application cards are another technique for assessing skill in application and performance. Faculty give students an index card and direct them to jot down one real-world application for what they have learned after students have studied an important theory, procedure, or principle. Application Cards encourage students to connect newly learned material with prior knowledge by getting students to think about possible applications. This technique allows students to see first-hand the relevance of their knowledge.[16]

Application cards develop several abilities: to make inferences from observation, to think for oneself, to apply principles to novel situations/problems, and to learn both theories and concepts in any subject. This technique lends itself most readily to upper-level courses. Students in introductory courses in Religious Studies may have difficulty doing application cards.

Here are some hints for using application cards effectively:

1. Choose a clearly applicable procedure or principle that your students are learning.
2. Only ask for two to three applications and give students three or four minutes to complete the exercise.
3. Tell your class to make up their own applications as opposed to writing down applications they have heard or read about.
4. Allow students in introductory courses to work in dyads or small groups in completing this exercise.

[16] Ibid., 236–239.

5. In turning the data collected into useful information, write "E" for excellent, "F" for fair, and "M" for marginal on each application card. Share with the class three of the best applications and three of the marginal ones. Students often learn as much from the work of their peers as they do from the instructor's examples.

6. It is important that students who suggest inappropriate applications receive feedback. Make sure they hear about correct applications so that the bad examples are not the only ones that stay with them.

7. If you have a few minutes at the end of your lecture, ask students to jot down two to three applications of what they have learned. To see first hand the relevance of what students are studying may very well increase both motivation to learn and student interest.

Another technique for assessing skill in application and performance is student-generated test questions. I have used this technique several times over the past two years with excellent results. Student-generated test questions are multi-purpose: they tell faculty what content students see as most important; they alert faculty to inaccurate expectations students have about examinations, and they give faculty a notion of how well students can answer questions they have posed.

In their book, *Classroom Assessment Techniques*, Thomas Angelo and Patricia Cross recommend administering student-generated test questions two to three weeks before a major test.[17] I have used student-generated test questions as a major test itself, making it count for 20 percent of a student's final grade. Students spent a great deal of time preparing test questions and answering them. Based on student feedback, I would have to say that student-generated test questions are a first-rate learning tool.

I have used student-generated test questions in a History of Christianity course. In this course I assign a ten-point quiz, which I devise, and then ask students to make up a mid-term exam based on the course content. Part of the exam is objective (multiple-choice, fill-in-the-blank, or matching questions), and part of it consists of either essays or short answers. The reason I assign student-generated test questions is this: many students complained about the examination I made up. In the process they learned how difficult and time-consuming it is to generate a good test.

I have used this technique with classes of ten to fifty students. For classes with more than fifty students, I recommend assigning specific chapters of the book/lectures to particular groups of students (such as

---

17 Ibid., 241.

the cooperative learning groups discussed in Chapter Six of this book).

I asked my students to make up a final exam for a seminar on critical thinking and the academic study of religion. I have included the final exam written by Jack Arnold, a religion major at Auburn, to show what students can achieve when making up student-generated test questions.

Final Exam for Seminar on Critical Thinking
Multiple Choice questions from the book:

1. According to chapter 6 on cooperative learning, the teacher should function as a _____, placing greater attention on listening rather than merely lecturing.
    a.   companion
    b.   mediator
    c.   judge of ideas
    d.   friend
    ANSWER: B

2. Of the following, which is the greatest barrier to critical thinking?
    a.   Students are not willing to learn
    b.   Professors are not supportive of one another's innovations
    c.   There is simply not enough time
    d.   Critical thinking cannot be taught
    ANSWER: C

3. _____ defines critical thinking as "a means to be careful or meticulous in examining our own thinking and that of others in order to improve our understanding."
    a.   Peter Facione
    b.   Richard Penaskovic
    c.   Joanne Kurfiss
    d.   Thomas Aquinas
    ANSWER: B

4. Which of the following is not presented in chapter three as important skills to learn?
    a.   Passive learning
    b.   Self-evaluation
    c.   Time management
    d.   Goal setting
    ANSWER: A

5. According to chapter nine in the book, _____ thinking is thinking in which ideas come bubbling up from the springs of creativity in one's mind. This type of thinking does not aim for control or conscious direction.
   a. second-order
   b. metacognitive
   c. critical
   d. first-order
   ANSWER: D

6. All but one of the following strategies helps students to learn in the active mode.
   a. the use of questions
   b. in-class writing exercises
   c. standard lecture
   d. cooperative learning
   ANSWER: C

7. Which of the following was not used in the book to define metacognition?
   a. Using control strategies in thinking
   b. The ability to evaluate arguments
   c. Thinking about one's thinking
   d. Dispositions of thoughtfulness
   ANSWER: B

Multiple choice questions from the presentations:

8. According to Stone's Rainbow Theory of cognitive development, the three tracks of development are:
   a. Theological, inspirational, leadership
   b. Religious, social, personal
   c. Philosophical, interpersonal, inspirational
   d. Theological, educational, leadership
   ANSWER: D

9. The move towards the acceptance of more than one religious path as true and towards valuing the contribution of all religions is called:
   a. Natural theology
   b. Fundamentalism
   c. Religious Pluralism
   d. Unitarianism
   ANSWER: C

10. Who wrote of woman that, "woman is a misbegotten man?"
    a. Tertullian
    b. St. Augustine
    c. Thomas Aquinas
    d. Elizabeth A. Johnson
    ANSWER: C

11. According to reformation theology, the state of man's soul at birth is best described as a state of:
    a. Free-will
    b. Total Depravity
    c. Goodness
    d. Occasional sin
    ANSWER: B

12. What is the official name of Auburn's version of Total Quality Management?
    a. Complete Quality Management
    b. Continuous Quality Management
    c. Educational Quality Management
    d. Immediate Quality Management
    ANSWER: B

13. Thomas Berry, who is the leader of a movement in Environmental Theology, has been called a Cultural Historical Theologian, but calls himself a:
    a. Geologian
    b. Environmental Theologian
    c. Theologian
    d. Ecologian
    ANSWER: C

14. The first stage of William Perry's Stages of Intellectual Development in which all information is evaluated as true or false and in which the authority of experts and textbooks is accepted without question is called:
    a. Dualism/Received Knowledge
    b. Multiplicity/Subjective Knowledge
    c. Dogmatism/Accepted Knowledge
    d. Relativism/Procedural Knowledge
    ANSWER: A

15. _____ believes that the divinity of Christ is a myth; according to this writer, Jesus was unique but not necessarily divine.
    a. Paul Knitter
    b. Raimundo Panikkar
    c. John Hick
    d. Stanley Samartha
    ANSWER: C

16. The two parts of the Constitution used primarily to set up the wall of separation between church and state in the U.S. are:
    a. Article 6 and the First Amendment
    b. Article 2 and the Third Amendment
    c. Article 5 and the Eighth Amendment
    d. Article 6 and the Fourteenth Amendment
    ANSWER: A

17. According to the presentation on marital violence, the religious groups that are typically most violent within marriage are:
    a. Fundamentalist Christians, Buddhists, Muslims
    b. Fundamentalist Christians, Muslims, Conservative Jews
    c. Muslims, Christians, Reformed Jews
    d. Fundamentalist Christians, Orthodox Jews, Muslims
    ANSWER: D

18. Who said, "The Bible does not condone wife-beating, it is faulty human interpretation that does?"
    a. Paul Knitter
    b. Billy Graham
    c. Rev. James Nichols
    d. Thomas Aquinas
    ANSWER: C

Fill in the blank questions from the text and the presentations:

19. _____ refers to an author's unstated agenda or motivation that makes the author subjective.
    ANSWER: Bias

20. The barrier to critical thinking called _____ refers to the fact that there is a great amount of declarative material that must be covered in a quarter.
    ANSWER: Coverage or Inadequate Time

21. There are two types of motivation, intrinsic and internal motivation and _____ motivation.
    ANSWER: extrinsic

22. There are three levels of knowledge which are interconnected. Among these are declarative knowledge and procedural knowledge. The third level of knowledge is _____ knowledge.
    ANSWER: metacognitive

23. According to chapter five, _____ occurs when students do something besides listening to the teacher, and this mode of learning assumes that students have a positive contribution to make in the learning process.
    ANSWER: Active Learning or Learning in the Active Mode

24. _____ , the author of *Toward a World Theology*, is a believer in the value of all religious paths.
    ANSWER: Wilfred C. Smith

25. There are two prominent groups in feminist theology: those that feel the church is irreparable and wish to leave it and those who feel change should be brought about from within the church. The second group are known as _____.
    ANSWER: Reformists

26. _____ may occur on three levels, the literal or verbal level, the feeling level, and the fantasy level.
    ANSWER: Listening

27. _____ was the 1962 Supreme Court decision which out-lawed mandatory prayer in school.
    ANSWER: Engle v. Vitale

28. _____ is the heart and soul of creative learning. It may be called "the clarifying companion to all other learning activities." It is a complex intellectual process central to both creative learning and proficient communication.
    ANSWER: Writing

29. Paul Knitter proposes the creation of a _____ in which there is a paradigm shift from Christ-centeredness to God-centeredness in Christianity.
    ANSWER: Theocentric

30. According to Joanne Kurfiss there are two parts of critical thinking: the "context of justification" and the "context of _____."
    ANSWER: discovery

31. The new area of religious thought (led by Thomas Berry) that calls for a new story of creation is called the _____.
    ANSWER: New Cosmology

32. _____ is the first step in Total Quality Management.
    ANSWER: Customer Focus or Customer Satisfaction

33. According to Martin Luther, the only reliable source of knowledge about the nature of God is (Latin please) _____.
    ANSWER: Sola scriptura

The final technique to be discussed relative to the assessment of skill in application and performance is the paper/project prospectus. The estimated level of time and energy required by students and faculty in using this technique is high. The paper/project prospectus tests students' skill at synthesizing their knowledge of a topic as they devise their own learning papers/projects. This technique gives faculty important information about three areas: students' planning skills, understanding of the assignment, and knowledge of the topic.[18]

The paper prospectus makes students reflect on the topic, audience, major questions of the term paper, basic organization, and time and resources required. The following example will give you some insight in the organization of a paper prospectus:

Prospectus for a Term Paper

Directions: Give a brief answer to each of the following items. This prospectus is only a plan, one that you will modify in the process of actually writing your term paper.

Proposed title:

Major question(s):

Purpose   (What do you hope to achieve?):

Schedule   (When will you do the paper?):

Outline   (of major sections):

---

[18] Ibid., 248. For a succinct treatment of making assessment work in the classroom, see Richard J. Stiggins, *et al*, *Measuring Thinking Skills in the Classroom* Revised Edition (Washington, D.C.: National Education Association, 1988), 23–27.

Resources needed:

Your major questions about completing this assignment:

By having students work through the paper prospectus, I find that students are more likely to jump right into the assignment rather than engaging in procrastination. The paper/project prospectus develops the ability of students to integrate ideas and synthesize information, it helps improve their writing and organizational skills and develops students' study skills and habits.

For those faculty who oversee fieldwork projects and plan student internships, I recommend the project prospectus, which is very similar to the paper prospectus. The following example sheds light on working up a project prospectus.

Project Prospectus

Directions: Answer each prompt with a short answer. This prospectus is only a plan, one that will be modified as you engage in the actual project.

Project Description   (What will you do?):

Setting   (Where will you work and with whom?):

Goal   (What questions will you answer?):

Resources needed, if any:

Timetable:

Your biggest fear about doing this project?

Summary

This chapter focused on assessment in terms of improving the teaching/learning process. In order to assess student learning, one must identify one's teaching goals. In formulating one's teaching/learning goals, we suggested that faculty use the Teacher Goals Inventory and Self-Scoreable Worksheet developed by Angelo and Cross.[19]

The bulk of this chapter examined various classroom assessment techniques such as the one-sentence summary; directed paraphrasing; classroom assessment projects; the defining features matrix; the pro and con grid; the content, form, and function outline; the analytic memo; application cards; student-generated test questions; and the paper/project prospectus. Various ways of using these techniques in sundry courses in Religious Studies were suggested.

[19] Ibid., 393–397.

8

Unsolved Mysteries

"I love to lose myself in a mystery, to pursue my Reason to an O altitudo."

Sir Thomas Browne

Introduction

There is a difference between the theory connected with critical thinking and related topics (as active learning, cooperative learning, and decision-making) and the actual classroom praxis. In this chapter I want to remark on integrating critical thinking into the academic study of religion.

This chapter revolves around these questions: How would one design a course in Religious Studies that emphasizes critical thinking as opposed to the traditional way of organizing a course? What practical difficulties does one encounter as one tries to do this? And how does one tie together the various strategies or techniques—active learning, cooperative learning, and the like—we discussed in this book?

This chapter begins by speaking to the issue of creating a climate for thinking, such as using the name-tag exercise, making students active in the process of learning, making a small beginning, encouraging students to be tolerant, and stimulating language use at all levels. Two fundamental points underline these: the implementation of critical thinking begins with the course syllabus, and faculty should use real-world problems because they make it easy for students to see the connection between their academic knowledge and their experiences in the real world.

Several suggestions are given in this chapter for structuring the classroom for thinking and designing group work. There is a brief discussion concerning the problem of transfer, followed by some hints on developing a thinking attitude. To encourage critical thinking, faculty must decide what are the important skills they want students to learn in their particular discipline. This chapter concludes by examining some problem areas and considering the benefits attached to infusing critical thinking into the academic study of religion.

The Difficulty

It is difficult to bring critical thinking into courses in Religious Studies when faculty have as their goal to help students learn all the facts about religion they can. It is like bringing in a new software program that faculty and students are to learn in an hour. The difficulty consists in this: there are no pre-packaged programs for infusing critical thinking into religious studies.

I suggest that faculty need to re-structure the same content they have been teaching in order to infuse critical thinking into their classes. Once faculty embark on this road there is no turning back. Teaching for critical thinking will then suffuse their teaching as sunlight penetrates a glass-enclosed room. Faculty will constantly refine their teaching as they feel more and more comfortable with this new way of teaching.

Create a Climate For Thinking

From day one I tell students that one of the purposes of the course is to get them to think for themselves. That way I clue them to the fact that thinking in my classes is a highly valued activity. Faculty set the tone for what happens in the classroom. It is not only by what faculty say that the tone is set, but also by how faculty act. I find it important to set a warm, welcoming environment in which divergent thinking is allowed. How is this done? I tell students outright, "If you disagree with me, you have something to give me." I then back this up by allowing students to challenge me and my interpretations of religion or theology.

One concrete way to create a warm atmosphere is the name-tag exercise, which students complete on the second day of class. They divide a sheet of paper into six sections. The first box asks for a "weather report" of how they are feeling that day: clear, cloudy, or rainy. The second box requires them to list three individuals who have been influential in their lives. The third box asks students to list three geographical locations that are important to them, such as their hometown, favorite vacation spots, or places that are meaningful to them in some way. The fourth box asks them to list three ideal jobs. In the fifth box they list five words describing themselves. The sixth and final box requires them to list three activities they cherish in ranked order. Students then share their responses in their small permanent group. This exercise goes a long way in building group cohesion.

Weather Report	*3 Influential Persons*	*3 Locations*
	1. Gervase Beyer	1. Munich, Germany
	2. John Henry Newman	2. Jersey shore
	3. Joe Doino	3. Gulf Shores

3 Ideal Jobs	5 Words To Describe You	3 Cherished Activities
1. Writer	warm, friendly,	1. basketball
2. Counselor	sincere, critical	2. reading
3. Research Scholar	athletic	3. listening to Bach

Some General Remarks

Once a warm atmosphere has been created in the classroom, several principles should guide activity.

1. Make students active in the process.   The single most important idea in the cognitive revolution and its applications to instruction has to do with active cognitive processing. Faculty in religious studies should have this mind-set as they design, implement, and evaluate their courses: How can I involve students in the learning of religious studies? As faculty plan their curricula, they need to remember to design group work on projects that involve class members working as a team to solve a concrete problem or to make a group presentation and on day-to-day assignments in class.

2. Begin small.   I recommend that faculty begin by making a series of small changes in their teaching in order to infuse critical thinking into religious studies. Start with a course that you teach on a regular basis and one that you feel comfortable with. There is a certain amount of risk-taking associated with changing one's teaching style and this will minimize one's risk. It is wrong to believe that only young faculty members innovate while older professors prop themselves up with dated, tattered notes. I would argue that the very opposite is the case. Neophyte teachers are more closely tied to their notes than experienced teachers. The freedom to redirect classroom time and to innovate presupposes control of one's subject matter.[1] This control is step one toward the effective teaching of any subject, but especially the effective teaching of thinking skills in the context of a specific discipline such as religious studies.

Begin by asking yourself this question: How can I re-structure this material in such a way as to maximize student involvement and learning? What kind of in-class assignments can I give that force students to think about the material presented? Many faculty believe in having students come to terms with the primary texts themselves. In teaching "The History of Christianity," I use the textbook by Van Voorst, *Readings in*

---

[1] Carol Lynn H. Knight, "Teaching Critical Thinking in the Social Sciences," *New Directions For Commmunity Colleges* 77 (Spring, 1992), 64.

Christianity. How can one use this text and still teach for critical thinking? Here are some suggestions that worked for me:

a. Have students read the excerpt from St. Augustine and paraphrase it in three or four key points. Then have them read their summary of Augustine to the whole class. One can then have a discussion of the key issues summarized by the group.

b. Have another group critique and check their summary of Augustine for accuracy. Did they omit any key ideas? Were they on target with their summary? Was the summary succinct and clear? Did they explain any technical vocabulary?

c. Another small group may grapple with this question: To what extent is the problem addressed by St. Augustine still a relevant theological concern today? If so, why so? If not, why not?

3. Think of it as easy.   A psychologist at the turn of the century, Emile Coue, was wont to say, "Think of what you have to do as easy, and it will become so." In many ways one may teach critical thinking in a similar way to how one taught before—with this difference: one must pay *explicit* attention to the skills level and to the metacognitive implications of what one teaches. What does this mean? A few examples are in order.

In a History of Christianity course students put on a project that involved a debate between St. Augustine and Pelagius on the subject of grace. Each disputant stated his or her position for five minutes, followed by rebuttal and counter-argument. Then the class joined in and asked questions of each protagonist. At the end of the session I asked students to answer this question: How was this debate a learning experience for you? Such a question forced students to think about the metacognitive implications of what they just experienced.

Another example: after returning the results of the first quiz to students I ask the class as a whole to reflect with me on this question: How can you do better the next time on the test's essay questions? Here are some of the responses:

a. Make a rough outline of your answer on scrap paper so that your essay is well structured and well organized. Why is this necessary? Because students' responses often have little logical organization and thus their argument lacks coherence and fire-power.

b. Pay close attention to the way the essay question is formulated. For instance, I asked students on the quiz to write a short biography of St. Augustine, paying special attention to his major writings. Many students did not comment on any of Augustine's writings. Others commented on *The Confessions* but failed to mention such obvious

candidates as *The City of God* and the *De Trinitate*. I also tell students
to avoid the shotgun approach and instead answer only the question asked without throwing in extraneous details that are not
related.

  c. Pay attention to language and its precise usage. If the question asks
for comment on the formation of the New Testament canon, begin
by stating exactly what is meant by a "canon." The class also suggested that students carefully read over their essays before turning
them in. Often there is a gap between what students actually said
on an essay and what they meant to say.

4. Encourage students to be tolerant. Critical thinking involves becoming
aware of our own biases, assumptions, and pre-judgments or prejudices.
We all look at reality through a particular lens. Our view or *Blick* of reality is colored by our environment, family, tradition, and values that we
have absorbed from the significant others in our lives. To think critically
means that we are open to the possibility that our own view of reality
may be distorted.

5. Stimulate thinking and language use at all levels. There are many ways
to organize and interpret information ranging from the simple levels
of knowledge and comprehension to more complex application, analysis, evaluation, and synthesis. Most faculty in religious studies are more
concerned with the simple levels of knowledge and comprehension
than with stimulating the development of higher-order thinking skills,
as we saw in Chapter Three of this book. Students must be challenged
with teaching approaches that stimulate various levels of cognitive functioning.[2]

6. Start cooperative learning immediately. I tell students on day one that
this class will probably be quite different from the traditional classes
they have. For one thing, there will be a lot of small-group interaction.
For another, I will not lecture more than twenty minutes at a time. If students are uncomfortable with this, I suggest that they sign out of my
course. However, less than a handful exercise this particular option.

    I break students up into small groups the first day of class. One prob-
lem with this is that some students may not actually sign into the course
until four or five days into the term because their financial aid did not

[2] John Chaffee, "Teaching Critical Thinking Across The Curriculum" *Critical Thinking:
Implications for Teaching and Teachers. Proceeding of the 1991 Conference.* eds. Wendy Oxman,
et. al. (Upper Montclair, N.J.: The Institute for Critical Thinking, 1992), 128.

come through in time. This presents a problem if the cooperative learning groups have already been formed. However, the problem is not as large as it appears. Inevitably, there will be some students who will drop the class because of scheduling difficulties. Thus there will be groups that consist of only four members rather than five. Newcomers can then take the place of those who dropped out of a group. If four individuals are new to the class, they can form a new group. On the course outline I make allowances for this new group by already assigning it a group project.

The Course Syllabus

The implementation of critical thinking commences with the course syllabus. Instead of handing out a finished syllabus on the first day of class, I first try to ascertain what the students' goals are for the course. This may take a few days. In the first week of class I have students do an exercise called goal ranking and matching.

Faculty often make one of three assumptions: that students have no course goals, that their goals for a course and that of the students overlap, that students' goals for a course are irrelevant and should play no role in the construction of the course syllabus.I would argue that most students do have course goals but are unable to make them explicit unless they are asked to do so. Based on my experience over the past five years in teaching critical thinking, I would say that knowledge about students' goals is most helpful to faculty in planning, teaching, evaluating, and improving their courses. My students seem to learn more if they can make connections between their course goals and the course requirements.

Goal ranking and matching gives students the opportunity to articulate their course goals and to rank them in terms of their importance. This exercise has several benefits: (1) it encourages active learning at the start of each course; (2) it makes students responsible for their own learning; (3) it increases student motivation and enthusiasm for a course by making connections between students' personal goals and course goals and, on occasion, by incorporating student goals into the course syllabus; and (4) it allows students to clarify their own learning goals, which is an important lifelong learning skill.[3]

Goal Ranking and Matching

The following suggestions are a helpful procedure to use in implementing goal ranking and matching:

---

[3] Thomas A. Angelo and K. Patricia Cross, *Classroom Assessment Techniques: A Handbook for College Teachers*, Second Edition, (San Francisco: Jossey-Bass Publishers, 1993), 290–294.

1. Work up clear and specific instructional goals for the course yourself before asking students to do this exercise.

2. Have students write down on a piece of paper five course goals without putting their name on the paper. Tell them that by "goals" you mean specific items they are to learn as a result of taking this course.

3. After listing their course goals (which should take no more than five minutes) have students rank the goals in the order of their importance for their lives. Have them put their rankings on the right of the goals on their list. Collect the data and tell students what you will use the results for and when you will discuss their responses.

4. In analyzing student responses look for patterns, recognizing similarities despite different ways of making the point. Compare student goals with your own instructional goals for the course, noting truly original or unique goals and categorizing them as such.

5. Then determine whether or not you want to incorporate some of the students' goals into your course outline. Be forthright in telling students which goals you cannot incorporate and why. I have found that I am often able to incorporate students' goals into the course by having them do research on a topic they are particularly interested in.

Use Real-World Problems

In teaching for critical thinking I try as much as possible to incorporate real-world problems into my courses. There are several advantages attached to using real-world problems. First, they often lend themselves to more than one correct answer. Hence, they are worth thinking about. Second, real-world problems often involve more than one content area. Hence they mirror the interdisciplinary nature of learning typically found in the real world.

Third, real-world questions draw on students' academic knowledge so that students easily see the connection between their academic knowledge and the real world. One does not have to worry about making one's course relevant when it addresses real-world problems. Fourth, students naturally become actively engaged in learning because their interest level in real problems is high. Fifth, real-world problems demand thoughtful judgment, organization, and collaboration. They automatically force students to engage in higher-order thinking.

When it comes to religious studies there are no shortages of real-world problems. Questions about abortion, contraception, pre-marital sex, God, the morality of war, physician-assisted suicide, and genetic engineering pique students' curiosity. Religion also deals with such perennial metaphysical questions as "How did the world begin?", "Why is there some-thing rather than nothing, when nothing is simpler than something?" and "What will become of us?"

Key variables that must be addressed have to do with the size of the class, how often the class meets, whether or not one is on the semester or the quarter system, how many majors are in the class, and how long a class session lasts. As a rule of thumb, the smaller the class, the easier it is to implement critical thinking. The larger the class, the harder it is to make every student happy. At the same time, the larger the class, the more important it is to use cooperative learning.

How to Structure the Classroom for Thinking
In this context "structuring" describes the way faculty control human energy, materials, space, and time in the classroom. Every teacher in every classroom structures those resources directly or indirectly. Even the so-called unstructured classroom has a structure within which stu-dents interact. Research shows that a well-structured classroom (where students use time efficiently, the teacher gives clear directions, and stu-dent energies are focused on a meaningful goal) produces high student achievement.[4]

The following section looks at three aspects of teacher structuring: 1. the clarity of written and verbal instructions; 2. the structuring of energy and time; and 3. structuring classroom organizational patterns for thinking.

Instructional Clarity
Students spend a lot of time and energy trying to figure out what teach-ers want and expect from them. Faculty must tell students outright that thinking is the goal of instruction, that they have the responsibility to think on their own, and that an answer may change when additional in-formation is added.

Students need to have clear directions about what they are expected to do in completing in-class or out-of-class assignments. Faculty should not provide too many details at one time nor should they keep repeating information that students already know. However, when the instructor uses different words to express the same idea or repeats concepts from

---

[4] See Arthur L. Costa, "Teacher Behaviors That Enable Student Thinking," *Develop-ing Minds: A Resource Book for Teaching Thinking*. ed. Arthur L. Costa (Washington, D.C.: Association for Supervision and Curriculum Development, 1985), 128ff. See Lowell Gish, "Classroom Climate for Critical Thinking," in *Critical Thinking: Implications for Teaching and Teachers: Proceeding of the 1991 Conference* eds. Wendy Oxman, *et al* (Upper Montclair, N.J.: Institute for Critical Thinking, 1992), 149–156.

one sentence to the next, students understand the directions better than if they were given just once.

It is important that students be given time to think about and synthesize what they are learning. I often have an open discussion (with the class sitting in one large circle) on how what we are learning this week relates to the students' lives or on the question "What are you learning in this class apart from subject matter?" I may have students write down in their notes the answers to these two questions, or I may break them into pairs to discuss their answers before they have a small-group discussion of this.[5]

Structuring Energy and Time
Students must on a regular basis receive instruction in cognitive skills. They must also face situations that force them to think throughout the school day. If this is done, then there is a greater possibility for application of that cognitive skill, generalization, and transference.

In and of itself, structuring time is insufficient to make students think. One must look at the extent to which students' energies are engaged. This is where cooperative learning and active learning fit in. Students must be given tasks to do in their courses in religious studies. In my classes, 40 percent of students' grades depends on how well they complete their in-class assignments. A large part of my job as instructor consists in devising meaningful in-class assignments that force students to come to terms with the course content.[6]

Structuring Classroom Organizational Patterns for Thinking
The key word in this connection is flexibility. Students have a need for a variety of classroom organizational patterns. In my experience some students, usually less able ones, require a great deal of structure. Others, often more capable students, need less structure since they are often internally motivated to learn on their own and have the basic skills necessary to work and think independently.

Research in curriculum and instruction suggests that when critical thinking and creativity are the instructional objectives, students do well when they are in the driver's seat, i.e., when they set their own goals,

---

5 Ibid., 129. In order to develop student's strategic reading capabilities, see Karen Scheid, *Helping Students Become Strategic Learners: Guidelines for Teaching* (Cambridge, MA: Brookline Books, 1993), 21–47.

6 See Barbara Gross Davis, *Tools for Teaching* (San Francisco: Jossey-Bass Publishers, 1993) 213–221. "Designing Effective Writing Assignments," Barry K. Beyer, *Practical Strategies For The Teaching of Thinking* (Boston: Allyn and Bacon, Inc. 1987), 139–162 and John C. Bean, *Engaging Ideas: The Professor's Guide to Integrating Writing Critical Thinking, and Active Learning in the Classroom* (San Francisco: Jossey-Bass Publishers, 1996), 73–132.

when they decide how to solve problems, and when they figure out the correctness of an answer based on data they produced. Faculty who allow students to structure their own learning and who value internal as opposed to external rewards, use a variety of classroom organizational patterns. For instance, they have individual students working on their own on tasks requiring such cognitive skills as classification, comparison, and struggling by providing hints toward the solution of a problem.

These faculty also use groups working in a collaborative fashion and interdependently to complete a group task such as a debate, panel discussion, or problem-solving exercise. When students work together to complete a group task insist that each student be assigned a role such as team captain, recorder, reflector, and positive person, as mentioned in Chapter Five. It is also helpful and efficient if students are given a set amount of time to complete the task. That way they learn to use their time productively.

Finally, these instructors encourage total group engagement in group discussion, Socratic dialogue, or a strategy I call twenty questions. In this strategy students spend fifteen minutes thinking up questions to ask me in the large group. These are questions dealing with any aspect of the class. If I cannot answer a particular question off the top of my head, I tell students so. I then look up the answer and report back to the class.

In order to learn to think, students must be given opportunities for thinking. Faculty in religious studies must engage students in interacting individually, in cooperative learning groups, and in total groups with creative activities that students devise and evaluate themselves.[7]

Designing Group Work

There are at least two ways of proceeding in designing group work. First, one may have in the wings a number of class assignments worked up before the class actually begins. One may glean these from the various books that have been written about critical thinking and then tailor them to the academic study of religion.

Second, one may make up the various assignments as one goes, that is, day-to-day. I prefer the second method because I like to be spontaneous and I'm not always sure about what a class needs until I have actually met it and have had some experience with its members. I find that classes, much like individuals, have their own personalities, and it takes time to obtain a good read on a class, just as it takes time to get to know an individual.

Here are a number of fail-safe exercises designed to get students to think critically and work in a cooperative fashion:

7 Arthur L. Costa, 131.

1. Instead of lecturing, I run off my notes for the class, have them break up into their cooperative learning groups, and ask for further questions they have about my notes. For example, in a class on Hinduism, I asked students if the relationship of *shruti* to *smriti* was analogous to the relationship between scripture and tradition in Christianity. Of course, I first had to explain the relationship between scripture and tradition to those unfamiliar with it. Another option would be to ask students how the notes relate to their own lives.

2. I often prime the pump for learning by asking students to write whatever comes into their mind when they hear the word *God*. Or I may ask a series of questions about God, such as if God were a part of nature, what part of nature would God be? If God were a geometric figure, what geometric figure would God be? If God were an animal, what kind of animal would God be and why? My students think very concretely, and they find this exercise provocative. A variation on this theme would be to ask about the relationship between God and themselves: If you were a part of nature, what part of nature would you be—a mountain, a tree, the sea? If you were an automobile, what kind of auto would you be and why?

3. A key problem faculty face is this: making sure that students actually do the assigned reading. One way to do this and to instill critical thinking is to have students work individually on this task in class. Summarize the chapter in 5 or 10 key points, numbering your points from one to five or from one to ten, as the case may be. Then have the students break up into dyads and critique each other's points. In a large class (100 students) this takes the burden from the faculty of reading 100 responses. Yet it squarely puts responsibility for reading and summarizing the text on the student and is active learning at its best.

4. There are several variants on the above exercise, all of them designed to help students become critical thinkers. Ask students to detect the author's assumptions and goals in writing the piece, chapter, or argument. Students may also be asked to comment on the persuasiveness of the chapter. Or I may ask them to write a counter-argument to the one proposed by the author.

5. Whenever possible, have students grapple with the primary texts themselves. Instead of talking abut the *Mahabharata* or *The Lotus Sutra*, give students excerpts from these scriptures so that they can see for themselves what these primary texts say. There is no better way to become acquainted with the world scriptures than by first-hand acquaintance. In my evaluations students tend to give me high marks for allowing them to read the *Bhagavad Gita* and other

primary texts themselves. That way they can form their own opinion of the text rather than depending on my or the author's interpretation. Students gain self-esteem if I have enough confidence in them to allow them to wrestle with the texts themselves.

In trying to infuse critical thinking into religious studies I find that most of my time is taken up with thinking of in-class activities that students can do. In this connection the best advice I can give faculty is this: be willing to experiment. A few examples will show what I mean by this.

I recently taught a course on Buddhist spirituality. Instead of devising a course outline, I had students break up into groups of three and come up with their own course syllabus. Of course this takes time, but I am convinced that the process is more important than the product. I feel that students will remember this course the rest of their lives.[8]

Variations on a Theme

Try to vary the structure of the class so that you are not predictable. Students never know quite what to expect on any given day in my class. I may start off with a mini-lecture followed by working in a small groups, or I may have them work on an exercise in pairs followed by a large group discussion.

Intellectual Joy

One need not look upon the design of group work as a chore. One may see it, instead, as a challenge, one that engenders intellectual joy. I see the design of small-group work as an opportunity to exercise my ingenuity and creativity. I get a certain amount of intellectual joy out of coming up with well-thought-out exercises for the small groups to work on.

I also find the experience liberating; that is, I am not bound to lecture, but instead can put the time I would normally spend into working up a lecture into wracking my brain to come up with good group exercises. This stretches me in a way that preparing for lectures does not.

The Problem of Transfer

A basic question in the literature on critical thinking is this: Does learning the skills of argument enable a student to reason effectively in various disciplines? John McPeck in his book, *Critical Thinking and Education,* maintains that critical thinking is discipline specific and is hence not a generalized skill.[9] He suggests that skills used in math, for example, will not transfer to other fields or to daily activities. McPeck comes to this

---

[8] For some excellent ideas on designing a course syllabus, see Barbara Gross Davis, 14–19.

[9] John McPeck, *Critical Thinking and Education* (New York: St. Martin's Press, 1981).

conclusion because critical thinking for him depends on knowledge of what constitutes good reasons in a discipline. To know what constitutes good reason in a discipline requires extensive knowledge of the matter. For McPeck, instruction in critical thinking without a solid foundation of specialized knowledge plays down the complexities that underlie even common or everyday problems.

One may ask if arguments share common features across disciplines. Stephen Toulmin found six basic elements found in arguments on any subject: claims, data, warrant, backing, modality, and rebuttal. Fields use various kinds of backing to justify warrants as well as specific kinds of evidence to support claims and criteria used to evaluate evidence. Toulmin concludes that arguments cannot be measured against any universal standard. Rather, they must be evaluated against whatever kind of cogency can be asked for in a particular field. Therefore, students can learn the structural features of arguments, but they must also learn the standards of evidence for each field they study.

Almost all scholars agree that background knowledge of a topic is essential to good argument, but I would disagree, in part, with McPeck's analysis. McPeck overlooks the commonalities found across disciplines in the construction of arguments.

Perkins distinguished between two types of transfer: high road, which requires a conscious effort and low road, which happens automatically and which cannot be counted on to transfer skills to any large degree. Why not? Perkins would say that these skills are not used in a variety of areas.[10]

Perkins would have students practice in many areas to expand the possibilities for the application of thinking skills (low road transfer). He also advises instructing students in the deliberate acquisition of the general principles that are the basis of critical thinking skills (high road transfer).

Alma Schwartz believes that thinking skill instruction should be integrated into the curriculum. If this instruction is applied across the curriculum, students will then have a wide range of thinking skills to call upon when they face an everyday problem or a problem in another area of study.[11]

I would maintain that successful transfer demands more than exercising thinking skills in different settings. It demands the development of

[10] David Perkins, *Smart Schools: From Training Memories to Educating Minds* (New York: The Free Press, 1991), 124–125. On teaching for transfer, see Barry K. Beyer *Practical Strategies For The Teaching of Thinking*, 163–189.

[11] Alma Schwartz, "Critical Thinking Attitudes And The Transfer Question" *Thinking Skills Instruction: Concepts and Techniques*, eds. Marcia Heiman, et. al. (Washington, D.C.: National Education Association, 1987), 58–68.

critical-thinking attributes or dispositions, such as the tendency to build on the ideas of others, toleration of diversity, and seeking reasons. Instruction in thinking skills may not lead to the transfer of thinking skills to other life situations if these critical-thinking attitudes are absent. The transfer of specific skills are made easy when such attitudes are present.

Transfer and Critical Attitudes

Critical thinking needs to be facilitated, not taught. To facilitate such thinking, we need to ensure that good critical-thinking attitudes are developed. This is how the critical-thinking skills, once internalized, will transfer. We as educators have to serve as role models for good critical thinking. If we are tolerant of differences and show ourselves willing to build on the ideas of others, our students will notice this and try modeling this behavior on their own. If we try to be well informed, take into account the total situation, and look for alternatives, our students will also do these things.

Another way to encourage the transfer of critical-thinking skills is to encourage risk-taking. That is, we must encourage our students to adapt ideas to novel situations. I do this by down-playing my position as an authority figure and by encouraging students to do group or individual projects that stretch their creativity. For example, I had an architecture student make a Shinto temple out of popsicle sticks, and I encouraged a group to do a project on Eskimo religion in which they built an igloo in the classroom.[12]

On Developing a Thinking Attitude

At the start of class provide relevant examples to motivate students to consider the ideas that are presented. For instance, if the topic is theological ethics, point out the contemporary questions that have an ethical component, such as the assisted suicides overseen by Dr. Kevorkian, the controversy over the new abortion pill, and whether our intervention in Iraq is justified or not.

Tell students that knowing the facts about a religion is only step number one. They must also learn when to question the facts and how to relate them to other topics. These subsequent steps, such as application and synthesis, are the real marks of critical thought. It is, for example, harder to explain the effects of the Reformation on the development of Western Christianity than it is to list the key events of the Reformation in chronological order. Inform students that they will make more mistakes on solving problems that require thought because this involves more difficulty than does note memorization. Help students see difficult material as a challenge that they can meet as opposed to a frustrating task.

12 See David Perkins, *Smart Schools*, 126.

Give students time at the end of class to work together in their cooperative learning groups. Have them review specific material, noting the problems they encounter.

Focus on Discipline-Specific Thinking Skills
To encourage critical thinking one must decide what are the important skills you want students to learn in your subject area. For instance, in a History of Christianity or History of Religions course these would be some important thinking skills: inference, acts of comparison, analysis, deduction, questioning the sources of information and other attempts to persuade, cause-and-effect relationships among events, and the importance of time as an underlying dimension in everything that happens historically.[13]

I find that it is particularly important to pay attention to the controversies. Students are often given simple answers to complex problems. Encourage students to think beyond the information given them and to ask important questions in the history of religions.

Determine the Content/Skill Mix
Every discipline in religious studies involves a combination of the relevant facts, the "givens" of the discipline, and the skills or relevant operations. In teaching the New Testament exegetes want students to know such facts as the difference between literary criticism and form criticism. However, Scripture scholars also want their students to develop such skills as interpreting a text correctly. How does one achieve a healthy mix between the facts students are given and the required skills that constitute the aim of your course?

One way to answer this question is to imagine a graduate of your class. How much of that student's knowledge deals with the relevant facts (what you want him or her to know) and how much involves skills of operation (what you want him or her to do)? Then ask yourself this question: Is this the mix I want? The mix of facts and skills is an artificial construct very much at the discretion of the instructor.[14]

As I attempt to infuse critical thinking into the academic study of religion I find a need to convert some of my givens into problems. Why so? I

13 Diane Halpern, "Thinking Across the Disciplines: Methods And Strategies To Promote Higher-Order Thinking In Every Classroom" *Thinking Skills Instruction*, 72. See John R. Verduin, Jr., *Helping Students Develop Investigative, Problem Solving, And Thinking Skills In A Cooperative Setting: A Handbook For Teachers, Administrators And Curriculum Workers* (Springfield, Illinois: Charles C. Thomas, Publishers, 1996).

14 Gary A. Woditsch with John Schmittroth, *The Thoughtful Teacher's Guide To Thinking Skills*. (Hillsdale, N.J.: Lawrence Erlbaum Associates, Publishers, 1991), 135. See Robert J. Sternberg and Louise Spear-Swerling, *Teaching for Thinking* (Washington, D.C.: American Psychological Association, 1996).

find that students have a limited capacity for plain information. By developing students' skills, I develop in them a content appetite. What happens is this: students wind up begging me to lecture on a particular topic, and when I do they are all ears.

An example may demonstrate what I have in mind. In teaching the history of Christianity in the Middle Ages I spend two classes on Scholasticism and Thomas Aquinas, in particular. I have students analyze Aquinas' cosmological proofs for the existence of God by analyzing the text of the *Summa Theologica* itself. Students are then given a small-group project in which they summarize Aquinas' argument and figure out who influenced Aquinas, such as Aristotle (since we have already discussed his theory of potency and act) and then make inferences about Aquinas the man based on the excerpts they have read from his writings.

I may also ask students to compare Aquinas' style of writing to that of St. Francis in his *Canticle of the Creatures*. What happens is this: students seem to have a much larger capacity for information they have a *job* for, as opposed to plain information. In other words, these are the benefits associated with an inductive approach to learning in which students make their own discoveries. It does take more time to pose information as a product of operation rather than as a given. However, the rewards in terms of student learning easily make up for the initial difficulty in this new approach to learning.[15]

Use Think-Aloud Protocols

To model your own thought processes, use think-aloud protocols. Try thinking out loud when you are thinking in class or working a problem on the blackboard. Verbalize the information you are studying and the steps you are going through mentally in solving a problem. When faculty think out loud, they are able to give students a way of thinking about the material so students can better understand it.[16]

Some Problem Areas

In trying to infuse critical thinking into the academic study of religion, one encounters several areas that are problematical. Making students active learners undoubtedly puts more responsibility on students for their own learning. The instructor takes on new and different roles: mentor, facilitator, and resource person. Students are not allowed to become passive learners, and from this arrangement complaints arise from students that the course is more difficult than they anticipated.

15 Ibid., 138.
16 Diane F. Halpern, 74.

I find that persuading my peers about the benefits of using critical thinking is not that difficult. A lot depends on a number of factors such as how useful, challenging, and fun the instruction proves to be when critical thinking is a main goal of instruction. The fun part derives from students working with their peers in small groups, but this too can be a source of challenge and frustration.

Problems in Small Groups
Students are unaccustomed, for the most part, to working in a small group on a regular basis and need, periodically, to be coached on how to deal with interpersonal difficulties. In a group of four there may be friction between two students who are on opposite ends of the spectrum and disagree on practically every topic.

Once cooperative learning group in my class consisted of three men and one woman. One of the male students consistently put down the woman's contributions. I should have been more sensitive to ensuring that the group had a good mix in terms of race, age, sex, and prior achievement. I met with the coed and encouraged her to stay in the group. During the next class session I gave a short twenty-minute presentation on how to work together successfully in a small group. I gave students hints on working well together and elaborated certain rules. This was enough to ensure the successful functioning of this particular group.

As a rule of thumb I never move a person out of one group and into another. One student begged me to move her into another group. I refused to do so because (1) I did not want to set a precedent and (2) in the so-called real world we have to learn to deal with those who are difficult. I have elaborated several rules for the smooth functioning of cooperative learning groups:

1. *Accept what others may say and let it sink in instead of rejecting their ideas out of hand.* In other words I tell students to allow themselves to be challenged by ideas with which they may disagree. Try to see the kernel of truth in what others may say, and do not be overly quick to do battle.
2. *Remember that no one has a monopoly on wisdom and no one has a monopoly on stupidity either.* Two plus two is four even if an idiot says so. I also remind students of Thomas Aquinas' axiom, "Do not quote authorities, rather consider the truth of what they say." Let authority belong, then, to the voice of wisdom.
3. *Treat others as you yourself would want to be treated.* This means avoiding put-downs, ridicule, and sarcasm. Instead, treat peers as partners in a dialogue.

The main cause, however, of small-group failure is when students are unclear about the group task involved and how they should proceed in completing the assignment.[17]

Dealing With Student Resistance
There will inevitably be minor problems associated with cooperative learning. Some students have a difficult time working constructively with others. In teaching Eastern Religions I had a student who wanted to leave the class early, although the group task was not performed in a satisfactory way. This particular student was a negative person and gave the group a hard time. Her attitude toward me was different because she was very grade conscious.

Here is how I handled the situation. I met with her small group and pointed out that they had not performed the task in a satisfactory manner. I then gave them ten extra minutes to do the assignment. In future meetings I made it a point to sit in and monitor the workings of this particular group. My presence in the group forced this negative, resistant student to work effectively with others.

If one observes student resistance, one must then give that group special attention at least for a while. If the group had continued to experience frustration, I would then be forced to meet with the negative student and try to persuade her to change her ways. I might also have given a mini-lecture on the frustrations associated with small-group learning.

At the time of my lecture, I would ask the class to list three reasons why they are experiencing frustration in working together in their small group. I would then ask them what three things they could do to eliminate their frustration, asking them to consider two questions: What part of your frustration is positive and beneficial and what part is negative and detrimental to the working of the group?[18]

It does not take a genius to infuse critical thinking into the academic study of religion. One of the things that faculty can do to teach thinking is to improve their questioning skills. All teachers ask questions. Faculty must simply change their style of questioning, asking questions that involve higher-order thinking. This alone will allow students to make a quantum leap in their ability to learn the material.

---

[17] James L. Cooper, et. al., "Cooperative Learning in the Classroom" *Changing College Classrooms: New Teaching and Learning Strategies for an Increasingly Complex World* (San Francisco: Jossey-Bass, Inc., 1994), 87.

[18] Daniel K. Apple, *Process Education: A Handbook of Activities for Process Educators* (Corvallis, OR: Pacific Crest Software, Inc., 1996), 39.

Benefits Derived From Teaching Critical Thinking

I find that my teaching has become rejuvenated since I started to infuse critical thinking into my classroom. I now see the classroom as a large learning laboratory wherein I vary the conditions to see what results. At times, I use a journal to record student reactions to my new approach to teaching. Rather than look upon change as destructive, I remind myself of the words of John Henry Newman in his *Essay on Development* written in 1845: "In a higher world it may be otherwise, but, here below, to live is to change and to be perfect is to have changed often."[19]

Summary

This chapter involved a reflection on some of the practical difficulties involved in integrating critical thinking into the academic study of religion. At the outset of the course it is important to create a climate for thinking by making use of the name-tag exercise, which creates a warm, welcoming climate. In attempting to infuse critical thinking into the academic study of religion one should make small changes in one's teaching. Ask yourself this question: How can I re-structure this material so as to increase student involvement and learning?

One should begin cooperative learning immediately. I try to use cooperative learning groups for 60 percent of the time spent in class. Use real-world problems if you really want to hold students' undivided attention.

This chapter suggested several strategies for structuring the classroom for thinking, such as using a variety of classroom organizational patterns from individual to small-group to total group work. The instructor needs to spend time designing group work, that is, collecting a repertoire of assignments that students work on together in small groups.

In this chapter we looked at the question of transfer-asking whether or not learning the skills of argument enables students to reason effectively in various disciplines. To encourage critical thinking, faculty must decide what are the relevant skills they want students to possess.

Faculty will undoubtedly face obstacles as they attempt to teach critical thinking. Students are unaccustomed to working shoulder to shoulder in cooperative learning groups and will need insight into managing the frustration that results. After five years of infusing critical thinking into the academic study of religion, I find a new zest for teaching. I an able to encourage students to become independent, self-directed learners. It does not get any better than this.

---

[19] John Henry Cardinal Newman, *An Essay on the Development of Christian Doctrine* (Garden City, New York: Image Books, 1960), 63.

Appendix A

Glossary of Terms

Active Learning:	Occurs when students do something besides listen to the teacher.
Algorithm:	This is a problem-solving procedure that will always yield the solution to a particular problem provided that it is followed exactly.
Argument:	One or more statements that are used to support a conclusion. It involves a train of reasoning in which claims and supporting reasons are linked to establish a position.
Assessment:	A multidimensional way to observe and to judge, on the basis of criteria, the individual learner.
Assumptions:	Statements in an argument for which no proof or evidence is given. Assumptions may be either implicit or stated.
Attention Control:	The key ingredient to doing well on any task. Energy control and bracketing are parts of attention control.
Bias:	An unreasoned distortion of judgement; closed-minded, prejudiced or irrational rigidity.
Bracketing:	That part of attention control in which one banishes thoughts irrelevant to the task at hand.
Brainstorming:	A method for producing many possible solutions to problems.
Briefing:	Refers to the explanation of the goal in cooperative learning and how to attain it.
Chunk:	An extensive knowledge base of perceptual patterns. For a M.D. a cluster of symptoms is a chunk. For a scholar in religious studies key terms and the names of leading thinkers in the field are chunks.
Chunking:	A memory process in which a number of related items are stored and retrieved as a unit. This is supposed to facilitate memory.

Cognitive Style:	Refers to recurrent patterns in how a person processes information and approaches problems.
Collaborative learning:	This involves small groups of students working together and offering each other affective and cognitive support while solving a challenging problem. Collaborative learning and cooperative learning are synonyms.
Conclusion:	The statement or belief that the writer/speaker is proposing; the last step in a reasoning process.
Convergent thinking:	Thinking that demands one single correct answer to a problem/question.
Cooperative learning:	The instructional use of small groups so that students work together to maximize their own and each other's learning.
Criterion (criteria, pl):	A rule, standard or test by which something can be judged/measured. Critical thinking makes explicit the standards/criteria for justifiable behavior and thinking.
Critical thinking:	To be careful or meticulous in examining our own thinking and that of others in order to improve our understanding.
Data schemata:	The idea that knowledge is stored and retrieved in bundles or packets. Also known as "state schemata."
Debriefing:	Refers to the evaluation of one's experience in cooperative learning. The process of debriefing revolves around these questions: What happened? What are your feelings about the experience? And what does it mean?
Declarative knowledge:	Cognitive psychologists speak of this as "knowledge that" or "knowledge about". All declarative knowledge is stored or represented in memory in the form of propositions or networks of propositions. Also known as "propositional" or "factual" knowledge.
Deductive reasoning:	This involves using our knowledge of two or more premises to infer if a conclusion is valid.
Deep processing:	A learning skill that helps one consciously generate emotions and linguistic information about thoughts, mental images and sensations. It is a method used to highlight information learned, as a way of stimulating thought or as a way to memorize information.
Divergent thinking:	Thinking needed to generate many different responses to the same problem/question.
Emancipatory learning:	That type of learning in which students are encouraged to become independent, self-directed, life-long learners.

Energy control:	Concerns raising or lowering one's energy at will, e.g., using relaxation exercises to overcome test anxiety.
Enumeration:	That type of structure in which an author lists facts or events.
Evaluation:	Making a judgement based upon a set of internal or external criteria as distinguished from mere subjective preference.
Expertise:	Results from the gradual development of high-level schemes that enable experts to quickly categorize recurring patterns of information or "chunks."
Expressive writing:	Involves thoughts written for oneself as in a journal or diary. It is crucial for finding new insights.
Extrinsic motivation:	Involves some goal, incentive or reward extrinsic to the task.
Fallacies:	Mistakes or errors in the thinking process. An argument which fails to conform to the rules of good reasoning.
First-order thinking:	Does not aim at control or conscious direction. Instead, ideas come bubbling up from some hidden spring. First-order thinking is both intuitive and creative.
Free writing:	Involves the production of many ideas without deliberate thought or censorship. Free writing corresponds to first-order thinking.
Goal-setting:	Means setting a direction and then developing a plan to get there. It is an important skill because it increases the likelihood that a certain task will be completed.
Graphic organizers:	These are also referred to as "concept maps." It means to use spatial displays to organize information.
Heuristic:	A general strategy that is used to solve problems and make decisions. Although a heuristic does not always provide a correct answer, it is usually a helpful aid.
Higher-order thinking:	Requires learners to manipulate ideas or information in ways that transform their meaning. Higher-order thinking includes both procedural or how-to knowledge (skills) and metacognition.
Inductive reasoning:	This involves collecting observations that suggest or lead to the formulation of a conclusion or hypothesis.
Inference:	The act of passing from one or more statements considered as true to another, the truth of which is believed to follow from that of the former. Inference involves two skills: coming up with multiple alternatives for resolving a problem and the ability to draw conclusions.

Intrinsic motivation:	Arises from within the learner and includes such things as pleasure, power and satisfaction from accomplishing one's objective.
Learning:	The process whereby novices become more expert in a particular subject/discipline.
Lecture:	An extended presentation in which the instructor presents factual information in an organized and logically-sequenced way.
Learning strategy:	A complex plan one formulates for accomplishing a learning goal. Or, it is the application of one or more specific learning tactics to a learning problem, or the technique one uses to perform a learning skill.
Learning tactic:	Any processing technique one uses in service of the plan.
Long-Term memory:	This refers to the memory system that keeps or stores information over long retention intervals.
Lower-order thinking:	Occurs when learners are asked to receive factual information or to use rules and algorithms through repetitive routines. Another name for lower-order thinking is declarative knowledge. The word "lower" is not a pejorative term. The process of teaching students to think is a complex network of relations among declarative knowledge, skills and metacognition.
Metacognition:	A technical term in cognitive psychology for developing self-consciousness about one's own thinking processes. It is sometimes referred to as critical reflection or as a literacy of thoughtfulness. Metacognition involves such control strategies as making plans, setting goals, asking questions, taking notes, observing the effectiveness of one's effort and taking corrective action.
Metamemory:	This refers to one's knowledge about his or her memory system.
Pacing:	Estimating how long it will take to complete an activity.
Operational definition:	An explicit set of procedures that inform the reader exactly how to both recognize and measure the concept under consideration.
Paraphrase:	This means to restate an idea or concept in one's own words.
Passive learning:	Occurs when students listen to lectures and jot down the important points.
Power thinking:	Refers to the conscious control of how one thinks by feeding oneself positive self-statements. It is effective

in preparing for some difficult task, as a way of gaining some desired skill or as a way of evaluating how the day went.

Premises:
The statements or reasons that support a conclusion.

Prejudice:
A belief, judgment or viewpoint formed before the facts are known or in disregard of facts which contradict it.

Problem:
A gap between where the solver is (currrent state) and where the solver wants to be (goal state), and the means for closing the gap is ambiguous.

Problem solving:
In psychology problem solving refers to behavior and thought processes directed toward the performance of some intellectually demanding task, for example, a jigsaw puzzle. Problems differ both in the nature of the skills required to solve them and in their level of difficulty.

Procedural knowledge:
Knowing how to use declarative knowledge to execute a skilled performance, such as how to write a critical book review. It also includes knowledge of how information is obtained, analyzed and communicated in a discipline. Procedural knowledge and strategic knowledge are synonymous.

Process schemata:
These are procedures or ways of both processing and organizing information.

Proof:
Reasoning or evidence so certain as to demonstrate the truth of a conclusion beyond a reasonable doubt.

Reasoning:
The process of forming judgements, conclusions, or inferences from facts or premises.

Reasons:
The bases for thinking that a conclusion is true.

Resistance:
A strategy by which students avoid taking the risks they need to take in class. Resistance is a natural response to a challenging situation.

Schema:
The sum of what a person knows about a given topic or thing. The singular of schemata.

Schemata:
Knowledge structures associated with a specific state, event or concept. The way human beings organize their knowledge about the world internally.

Second-order thinking:
Conscious, controlled and directed thinking. It strives for control and uses logic and reason as its guides.

Self-evaluation:
The ability to assess the learning skills that a person possess.

Short-term memory:	This refers to the memory system that stores memory for a very short period of time, perhaps around one minute. This is also referred to as "working" memory.
Skill:	The ability to use knowledge, such as driving a car, writing a book review or teaching in a competent way.
Socratic questioning:	A type of questioning that deeply probes the meaning, justification or strength (logical) of a position or line of reasoning.
Stepping:	Means structuring the class so that students experience learning as a series of developments. Stepping is used to build a supportive climate in the classroom.
Strategy:	The art of devising plans toward the achievement of a goal.
Structure:	Refers to the way authors organize their ideas such as question and answer, thesis-proof, or statement of a problem followed by a solution.
Student-centered learning:	In this approach students assume responsibility for establishing personal educational objectives. The instructor becomes an explorer who provides a road map for the students' own journey of discovery.
Syllogism:	This is an argument whose conclusion is supported by two premises.
Syllogistic reasoning:	This is a form of reasoning in which one decides whether or not a conclusion can be properly inferred from two or more statements.
Teacher-centered learning:	The instructor decides unilaterally how the knowledge and skills will be imparted during the structured learning process.
Thinking:	Our active, organized effort to make sense of the world and to clarify our understanding. Thinking involves combining information stored in memory so that the end result is different from, and something more than, what was started with.
Thinking aloud protocols:	These are verbatim records of what a learner says or does while solving a problem. They are useful in formulating models of how individuals think.
Thinking styles:	These are ways of directing the mind that a person finds comfortable. Thinking styles are propensities rather than abilities, they are ways in which individuals prefer to use their intelligence.

Transfer:	Refers to learning something in one context or situation and then applying it in another situation, for example, putting the math one learns at school to work in building a wooden desk at home.
Transactional writing:	Is used to communicate facts and information.
Vertical thinking:	Logical or straightforward thinking. It is the opposite of "lateral thinking: and is used in the refine ment and development of ideas and solutions.

Select Annotated Bibliography

Note that some of the following books fall into more than one category. There is less of a problem with the journal articles since they are easier to categorize than are the books, some of which fit into practically every category listed.

Assessment of Critical Thinking

Angelo, Thomas A. "Classroom Assessment: Improving Learning Quality Where It Matters Most." *The Changing Face of College Teaching*. ed. Marilla D. Svinicki. San Francisco: Jossey-Bass, Inc., 1990: 71–82.
Assessment applies to a wide range of approaches used to measure educational effectiveness. Argues that faculty need explicit training to assess student learning. Before faculty can assess how well their students are learning, they must identify/clarify what they are trying to teach.

Angelo, Thomas A. and Patricia K. Cross. *Classroom Assessment Techniques: A Handbook for College Teachers*. 2nd ed. San Francisco: Jossey-Bass Publishers, 1993.
It is difficult to recommend this book on classroom assessment techniques too highly.

Berrenberg, Joy L. and Ann Prosser. "The Create-A-Game Exam: A Method to Facilitate Student Interest and Learning." *Teaching of Psychology* 18 No. 3 (October, 1991): 167–170.
The authors developed the create-a-game exam as part of a take-home exam in a senior level History of Psychology course. Students have two weeks to complete the exam and game, which is a challenging and effective alternative to traditional evaluation methods. The element of fun in this kind of exam motivates students to learn more than an exam that stresses rote memorization.

Bloom, B., et al. *Taxonomy of Educational Objectives*. White Plains: Longman, Inc., 1977.
The author distinguishes six main levels of thinking: knowledge, comprehension, application, analysis, synthesis and evaluation. One may use these levels of thinking to design test questions that measure higher-order thinking skills.

Carroll, Sarah M. and Daniel K. Apple. *Learning Assessment Journal*. Corvallis: Pacific Crest Software, Inc., 1995.
Loaded with practical exercises for the assessment of student learning. Extremely helpful to both novice and expert teachers.

Cromwell, Lucy S. "Assessing Critical Thinking." *New Directions For Community Colleges* Vol. 20, No. 1 No. 77 (Spring, 1992): 37–50.
The standard definition of critical thinking has shifted from the ability to recognize certain thought-patterns in the work of others to doing one's own critical thinking. Cromwell sees critical thinking as the ability to apply disciplinary frameworks in academic, personal and professional settings and to evaluate and monitor that activity. Assessment is an ongoing activity at the center of the learning process, not a test that comes at the end of learning.

Davis, Barbara Gross. *Tools for Teaching*. San Francisco: Jossey-Bass Publishers, 1993.
A wealth of material on different aspects of critical thinking especially the sections on leading a discussion, learning styles and preferences and designing effective writing assignments.

Eble, Kenneth E. *The Craft of Teaching*. San Francisco: Jossey-Bass, 1976.
Lists qualities of good teachers, has some excellent ideas about the lecture as discourse and has a good chapter on grades.

Facione, Peter A. "Testing College-Level Thinking." *Liberal Education* 72 No. 3 (Fall, 1986): 221–231.
Sees critical thinking as one's ability to present well-reasoned arguments and to evaluate correctly the arguments others present. Argues that critical thinkers are able to detect a person's hidden assumptions and presuppositions.

Haladyna, Thomas M. *Writing Test Items to Evaluate Higher Order Thinking*. Boston: Allyn and Bacon, 1997.
This book is a comprehensive guide to writing test items that measures important higher level student outcomes at all educational levels. The core of this book is the actual writing of test items, including multiple choice type questions. It represents the most complete discussion of the subject of item development I have ever read.

McDaniel, Ernest and Chris Lawrence. *Levels of Cognitive Complexity: An Approach to the Measurement of Thinking*. New York: Springer-Verlag, 1990.
This book describes a new approach to the measurement of thinking processes, viz., in terms of the processes used in interpreting situations. In this approach specific markers help define levels of thinking.

Nummedal, Susan G. "How Classroom Assessment Can Improve Teaching and Learning." *Changing College Classrooms*. ed. Halpern and Associates. San Francisco: Jossey-Bass, 1994: 289–305.
One of the key questions in assessment is this: What are my students learning in my classroom as a result of my instruction?

Rief, Linda and Maureen Barbieri, eds. *All That Matters: What Is It We Value in School and Beyond?* Portsmouth, New Hampshire: Heinemann, 1995.
This book contains various essays on testing and measurement and adds to the national debate on these issues. The essayists focus on various aspects of alternative assessment and make the point that evaluation should stress what students actually know, what they can do, and should point out areas for improvement. To evaluate, then, means to celebrate signs of growth.

Stiggins, Richard J., et al. *Measuring Thinking Skills in the Classroom: Revised Edition.* Washington, D.C. National Education Association, 1988.
The 32 pages that comprise this book are worth their weight in gold. The first section deals with measuring thinking skills, followed by a chapter on learning to plan the assessment and concluding with a section on making assessment work in the classroom. Particularly helpful is Appendix C on Cognitive Domain Levels according to Bloom. If one wants to measure synthesis, for example, then one can use such key words as: combine, relate, put together, integrate, assemble or collect.

Tye, Kenneth A. "Restructuring Our Schools: Beyond the Rhetoric." *Phi Delta Kappan* 74 No. 1 (Sept., 1992): 8–14.
Says that testing should be a way of diagnosing strengths and weaknesses in learning rather than a measure of accountability.

Barriers to Critical Thinking

Brown, Rexford. *Schools of Thought: How the Politics of Literary Shape Thinking in the Classroom.* San Francisco: Jossey-Bass Publishers, 1991.
Contains an excellent discussion of metacognition, the politics of literacy and cultivating a literacy of thoughtfulness.

Campbell, David N. "All Talk: Why Our Students Don't Learn." *Educational Horizons* 68 No. 1 (Fall, 1989): 3.
Argues that we learn permanently when an experience has meaning, when we make a connection to something else and when we integrate the new knowledge into existing understanding.

Collins, Cathy and John N. Mangieri, eds. *Teaching Thinking: An Agenda for the Twenty-First Century.* Hillsdale: Lawrence Erlbaum Associates, 1992.
The various essays in this book make the point that students will not become more thoughtful unless the improvement of thinking becomes the basic goal of higher education.

Ford, Patrick J., S. J. "Some Obstacles to Undergraduate Teaching." *Improving College and University Teaching* 25 (1977): 9–12.
Higher education would be helped by the development of a promotional system by which one adept at teaching would be permitted to teach with the assurance that evaluations and rewards will be based on

criteria essentially different from those on which the effectiveness of the research scholar is evaluated.

Gaff, Jerry G. "Beyond Politics: The Educational Issues Inherent in Multicultural Education." *Change* (Jan./Feb. 1992): 31–35.
Maintains that teaching and learning that occurs in multicultural courses is different from other types of general education courses. Two trends that will influence curriculum change in the 90's are: 1. multiculturalism and 2. the need to increase students' global awareness.

Cooperative Learning

Agne, Karen J. "Caring: The Expert Teacher's Edge." *Educational Horizons* 70 No. 3 (Spring, 1992): 120–123.
Argues that teachers succeed only when they can empower others. To do this presupposes commitment and deep caring.

Bosworth, Kris and Sharon Hamilton. *Collaborative Learning: Underlying Processes and Effective Techniques*. San Francisco: Jossey-Bass Publishers, 1994.
This volume looks at the processes underlying the collaborative learning paradigm. The nine essays that are presented in this book discuss the social skills needed for effective collaborative learning, and the current and future use of technology in collaborative learning classrooms with practical reference to electronic classrooms, interactive video, and hypermedia systems.

Carkhuff, Robert R. *The Art of Helping: A Guide for Developing Helping Skills for Parents, Teachers and Counselors*. Amherst: Human Resource Development Press, 1973.
A helpful guide for teaching students how to work cooperatively in a small group setting.

Cole, Robert W. and Philip C. Schlechly. "Teachers as Trailblazers." *Educational Horizons* 70 No. 3 (Spring, 1992): 135–137.
Maintains that the role of the teacher is to invent work at which students experience success, then to lead students in the direction of that success.

Cooper, James L., et al, "Cooperative Learning in the Classroom." *Changing College Classrooms: New Teaching and Learning Strategies for an Increasingly Complex World*. ed.Halpern and Associates. San Francisco: Jossey-Bass, 1994: 74–92.
Positive Interdependence is one of the critical features that distinguishes cooperative learning from other forms of small-group instruction. Has some excellent ideas on constructive controversy whereby pairs within a four person team are assigned different sides of an issue. Each pair researches one side of the topic. Pairs then switch sides and develop arguments for the opposite side of the same issue.

Cross, K. Patricia. *Accent On Learning*. San Francisco: Jossey-Bass, 1976.
    Excellent discussion on "cognitive styles" and "interpersonal skills."

Duncan-Hewitt, Wendy, David L. Mount and Dan Apple. *A Handbook on Coopera-
    tive Learning*. 2nd ed. Corvallis: Pacific Crest Software, Inc. 1995.
    This handbook contains many practical hints on the implementation of
    cooperative learning in higher education.

Hamm, Mary and Dennis Adams. *The Collaborative Dimensions of Learning*. Nor-
    wood: Ablex Publishing Corporation, 1992.
    Reports on different approaches to cooperative learning, and speaks to
    the difficulty of connecting writing, reading, thinking and learning. Has
    some good insights on adapting cooperative learning to the students of
    the 1990's.

Johnson, David W., Roger T. Johnson, and Karl A. Smith. *Cooperative Learning:
    Increasing College Faculty Instructional Productivity*. Washington, D.C.:
    George Washington University, 1991.
    This is one of the very best books on cooperative learning ever written.

Johnson, David W. and Roger T. Johnson. *Learning Together and Alone: Coopera-
    tive, Competitive and Individualistic Learning*. Boston: Allyn and Bacon,
    1987.
    The Johnson brothers have been perfecting their knowledge of coopera-
    tive learning for the past two decades.

Satir, Virginia. *Conjoint Family Therapy*. Palo Alto: Science and Behavior Books,
    Inc., 1967.
    Has an informative discussion of communication and its various di-
    mensions. Good as background for teaching cooperative learning skills.

Slavin, Robert E. *Cooperative Learning*. 2nd ed. Boston: Allyn and Bacon, 1995.
    The first part of this book gives readers the intellectual grounding for
    cooperative learning, i.e., the theory and research that underlie class-
    room practice. The second part gives "how to" information in the form
    of practical advice for dealing with such issues as the pitfalls of co-
    operative learning, the organization of one's time to ensure adequate
    coverage of the content, and the importance of explaining, demonstrat-
    ing, or reexplaining in the beginning stages what you expect students to
    accomplish.

Williams, Kimberly D. "Cooperative Learning: A New Direction," *Education* 117
    No. 1 (Fall, 1996), 39–42.
    This article reports on a new theory that tailors the basic concepts of co-
    operative learning to meet students' individual needs. Williams tries to
    identify learners by using four diverse categories: writer, speaker, artist,
    and researcher. This way of proceeding allows students to use their
    strongest talents across the curriculum, and promotes ways of im-
    proving their weaknesses. Although this method has worked well in
    History and English, it has yet to be proven for Religious Studies. How-
    ever, I am confident that it will work there as well.

Critical Thinking and Creativity

Bailin, Sharon. *Achieving Extraordinary Ends: An Essay on Creativity*. Dordrecht, the Netherlands: Kluwer Academic Publishers, 1988.
A philosophical analysis of creativity. Bailin explores the connection between originality and creativity, and argues that the originality of creative products can only be understood with reference to the traditions out of which they develop. Bailin believes that "significance" rather than novelty is the primary determinant of creativity.

Cropley, Arthur J. *More Ways Than one: Fostering Creativity*. Norwood: Ablex Publishing Corporation, 1992.
This book treats such topics as social and emotional blocks to creative thinking, helping students produce ideas and specific classroom activities for fostering creativity. Of particular significance is the section on the role of the teacher in fostering creativity.

Evans, James R. *Creative Thinking in the Management and Decision Sciences*. Cincinnati: South-Western Publishing Co., 1990.
Sees problem solving as a basis for creativity. Discusses the educational implications of creative thinking.

Gardner, Howard. *Frames of Mind: The Theory of Multiple Intelligences*. New York: Basic Books, Inc., 1983.
Gardner argues that intelligence is not a single capacity at all, but the ability to fashion products, or to solve problems that are of significance within one or more cultural settings. Gardner speaks of linguistic intelligence, logical mathematical intelligence, musical intelligence, bodily kinesthetic intelligence, spatial intelligence, interpersonal intelligence and intrapersonal intelligence.

Gruber, Howard E., et al. *Contemporary Approaches to Creative Thinking*. New York: Atherton, 1962.
These essays deal with various aspects of creativity. I particularly recommend the essay by Jerome Bruner on "The Conditions of Creativity."

Halpern, Diane. *Thought and Knowledge: An Introduction to Critical Thinking*. 3rd ed. Mahwah, New Jersey: Lawrence Erlbaum Associates, Publishers, 1996.
A good place to begin in trying to infuse critical thinking into one's courses. The author discusses the need for critical thinking skills, problem-solving, decision making and gives several strategies for creative thinking. There is a helpful chapter summary at the end of each chapter, a list of terms to know and suggested readings. It is difficult to recommend this book too highly.

Jones, Beau Fly and Lorna Idol, eds. *Dimensions of Thinking and Cognitive Instruction*. Hillsdale: Lawrence Erlbaum Associates, Publishers, 1990.
A wealth of material on critical thinking and an excellent essay by David Perkins on "The Nature and Nurture of Creativity."

Kirby, Dan and Carol Kuykendall. *Mind Matters: Teaching for Thinking.* Portsmouth: Boynton/Cook Publishers, 1991.
Contains many good questions about how to teach for thinking. Various chapters contain thoughtful essays on thinking like an artist, an inventor, a naturalist and thinking like an anthropologist.

Maslow, Abraham. *The Farther Reaches of Human Nature.* New York: Viking Press, 1971.
Maslow believes that the concept of creativeness and that of the healthy, self-actualizing fully human person may turn out to be the same thing. Maslow distinguishes between primary creativeness, the inspirational phase of creativity in which one becomes lost in the present, and secondary creativeness which depends on patience, stubbornness and hard work or the development and working out of the inspiration. Maslow argues that bright ideas take but a small proportion of our time, whereas most of our time is spent on hard work.

Miller, William C. *The Creative Edge: Fostering Innovation Where You Work.* Reading: Addison-Wesley Publishing Company, Inc., 1986.
This book contains sections on enhancing one's individual creative process, using intuitive techniques such as imagery, dreams, drawing, analogy, meditation and brainstorming for idea generation and institutionalizing innovation in the workplace.

Novak, Joseph D. and Bob D. Gowin. *Learning How to Learn.* Cambridge: Cambridge University Press, 1984.
Has an excellent discussion of "concept mapping." Discusses concept mapping as an evaluation tool. Recognizes that knowledge that increases human understanding is constructed, that claims from any one inquiry are just a brick or two in the construction of knowledge about education, and that some of this knowledge will be cast aside in later inquiries.

Oxman-Michelli, Wendy. "Critical Thinking As Creativity," *Inquiry: Critical Thinking Across The Disciplines* 9 No. 3 (April, 1992): 1; 21–26.
Critical thinking as creativity may be seen as a dialogue between the individual and one's creative work. Critical thinking and creativity may best be approached as two sides of the same coin—pennies perhaps.

Pagano, Alicia L. "Learning and Creativity." *The Journal of Creative Behavior* 13 No. 2 (Second Quarter, 1979): 127–138.
Speaks about the exciting relationship that exists between creativity and learning. Feels that every time we teach students something, we keep them from inventing it themselves. That which we allow students to discover by themselves will remain with them for the rest of their lives.

Penaskovic, Richard. "The Nexus Between Creativity and Critical Thinking: Applications To Religious Studies." *Critical Thinking: Implications for Teaching and Teachers. Proceedings of the 1991 Conference* ed. Wendy

Oxman, et al. Upper Montclair: The Institute for Critical Thinking, 1992: 342–348.

Part 1 of this essay examines the work of Sharon Bailin on creativity. Part 2 deals with the application of critical thinking skills to the academic study of religion. The author reflects on the axiom: "When it comes to learning, the perspective of the student counts the most."

———. "Toward a Definition of Creativity." *Essays on Creativity and Science*. ed. Diana Macintyre De Luca. Honolulu: Council of Teachers of English, 1986.

Creativity may be understood in five different ways: it may refer to an individual's potential for achievement, the act of creativity, or it may be applied to the intervening process by which one's behavior is directed toward a creative product, or one may speak of creativity as a product and finally, creativity may have reference to the individual person as such, that is, to creative persons and their characteristics.

Perkins, David N., et al. *The Mind's Best Work*. Cambridge: Harvard U P, 1981.

This book examines the notion of creativity particularly in the arts and sciences with products such as discoveries, paintings, poems and scientific theories. The author attends to puzzles of various sorts because they provide a controlled way of examining certain aspects of creativity. "Personal experiments" are a key feature of this book. These involve the reader in accomplishing a task with some sort of introspection into the workings of the mind, such as a puzzle or a problem to solve.

Sternberg, Robert J. *Wisdom: Its Nature, Origins, and Development*. Cambridge: Cambridge University Press, 1990.

One can distinguish wisdom, intelligence and creativity in terms of the six background variables that lead to the use of one particular term (rather than one of the others) to label a person. The six variables are: knowledge, cognitive processing, intellectual style, personality, motivation and environmental context.

Tuerck, David G., ed. *Creativity And Liberal Learning: Problems And Possibilities in American Education*. Norwood: Ablex Publishing Corporation, 1987.

Tuerck pursues such topics as ways of thinking about creativity, methods of teaching creativity, developing skills for creative thought and new directions in the teaching of creativity. Researchers cannot agree on what creativity means and this is seen as one of the biggest stumbling-blocks. The concept of creativity remains "a slippery beast."

Teaching in the Active Mode

Aaronsohn, Elizabeth. *Going Against the Grain: Supporting the Student-Centered Teacher*. Thousand Oaks, California: Corwin Press, Inc. 1996.

This book suggests that if practicing teachers have direct and continuous access to teacher educators for support while they work at discarding traditional assumptions, then those who dare to imagine student-centered teaching can work gradually toward implementing their vision. Many of the ideas found in this book may be transposed to teaching undergraduates, although this book is primarily addressed to secondary school teachers.

Baldwin, Jill and Hank Williams. *Active Learning: A Trainer's Guide*. Oxford: Blackwell Education, 1988
Contains many practical tips on creating a classroom environment conducive to active learning.

Bazerman, Charles and David Russell, eds. *Essays: On Writing Across the Curriculum*. Davis: Hermagoras Press, 1994.
Deals with writing across the curriculum as a challenge to rhetoric and composition. I particularly recommend the essay by Janet Emig "Writing as a Mode of Learning."

Bean, John C. *Engaging Ideas*. San Francisco: Jossey-Bass Publishers, 1996.
The author assumes that all significant learning takes its point of departure from the student's engagement with problems. One of the instructor's main tasks, then, is to design meaningful and interesting problems. This book should be read as a nuts-and-bolts guide that will assist faculty from any discipline to design provocative writing and critical thinking activities and incorporate them into respective courses. Some sample topics are: understanding the connection between thinking and writing, helping students read difficult texts, and enhancing learning and critical thinking in essay examinations.

Benjamin, Ludy T., Jr. "Personalization and Active Learning in the Large Introductory Psychology Class." *Teaching of Psychology* 18 No. 2 (April, 1991): 68–74.
Gives some great ideas for personalizing the large class in psychology. Many of these ideas may be used by faculty who teach large classes in religious studies.

Bonwell, Charles C. and James A. Eison. *Active Learning: Creating Excitement in the Classroom*. ASHE-ERIC Higher Education Report No. 1. Washington, D.C.: The George Washington University, 1991.
This is, far and away, the best book on active learning.

Elbow, Peter. *Embracing Contraries: Explorations in Learning and Teaching*. New York: Oxford University Press, 1986.
Distinguishes between first-order thinking and second-order thinking. Argues that the two writing processes enhance the two thinking processes. Contains many practical suggestions for teaching students to think using writing exercises.

Fulweiler, Toby. *Teaching With Writing*. Upper Montclair: Boynton/Cook Publishers, 1987.
Contains many helpful strategies so that students can learn to think critically by writing.

Hayes, John R. *The Complete Problem Solver.* 2nd ed. Hillsdale: Lawrence Erlbaum Associates, Publishers, 1989.
This book has two purposes: to provide the reader with the skills that make one a better problem solver and to provide up-to-date information about the psychology of problem solving. One finds excellent chapters on writing as problem solving, decision making and how social conditions affect creativity.

Hill, Clare Conley. *Problem Solving: Learning and Teaching: An Annotated Bibliography.* London: Frances Pinter (Publishers) Ltd., 1979.
Contains many helpful books on the various aspects of problem solving such as problem solving in restructuring problems, how problem solving can be encouraged by teaching styles and how problem solving is modified by individual differences.

Kersch, Mildred. "Integrative Curriculum for the 21st Century." *Educational Horizons* 68 No. 1 (Fall, 1989): 2–7.
Integrative learning gives students the opportunity to select their own organizing principle. Maintains that the integrative curriculum unties the knowledge bundles we call subject areas or disciplines seeking to unify a student's educational activities across subject matter boundaries.

Kutz, Eleanor, Suzy Q. Groden and Vivian Zamel. *The Discovery of Competence: Teaching and Learning with Diverse Student Writers.* Portsmouth: Boyton/Cook, 1993.
The writing classroom is not simply a place for certifying that some students can demonstrate the linguistic practices of the university, but a place where students may build on their competence and realize their possibilities as writers and learners.

Leahy, Richard. "The Power of the Student Journal," *College Teaching* 33 No. 3 (Summer, 1982): 108–112.
Have students record their reactions to the class sessions and to the outside reading on loose-leaf paper and put these in manilla folders. Entries should contain various strategies for learning such as summarizing, questioning, synthesizing and relating the subject matter to the writer's prior knowledge.

Litecky, Lawrence P. "Great Teaching, Great Learning: Classroom Climate, Innovative Methods, and Critical Thinking." *New Directions for Community Colleges* 77 (Spring, 1992): 83–90.
The author uses a formula for creating more active participation in the class. At the start he introduces the topic and describes what will occur for the balance of the period for seven minutes. Then he puts a discussion statement on the board and asks students to write a response for five minutes. Students then form groups of three or four to discuss their written responses for eight minutes. Comments are then invited from the group. Those in agreement with the statement give their reasoning and those opposed to the statement also give their reasoning.

Litecky believes that the exploration of assumptions, conclusions, definitions, evidence, language use and reasoning cultivates the best habits of the mind.

Lundsford, A. *The Presence of Others*. New York: St. Martin's Press, 1994.
Contains some excellent ideas on critical reading, on writing a position paper, keeping a reading log and working with sources. Includes guidelines for paraphrasing, quoting and summarizing sources.

Oxman, Wendy, Mark Weinstein and Nicholas M. Michelli, eds. *Critical Thinking: Implications for Teaching and Teachers*. Proceedings of the 1991 Conference. Upper Montclair: Institute for Critical Thinking, 1992.
Contains a number of short essays on various aspects of critical thinking.

Penaskovic, Richard and von Eschenbach, John. "Infusing Critical Thinking into the Academic Study of Religion," *Spotlight on Teaching* Vol. 7, No. 4 (November, 1992): 8–10.
This article reflects on the thinking-writing connection. If we want students to become critical thinkers then we must give them the opportunities to practice thinking, e.g., by writing, be it in a journal or by using in-class writing exercises.

Rabow, Jerome, et al. *William Fawcett Hill's Learning Through Discussion*. 3rd ed. Thousand Oaks: Sage Publications, Inc. 1994.
Contains many practical tips on learning through discussion, group members's roles and skills and the role of the instructor.

Schiever, Shirley W. *A Comprehensive Approach to Teaching Thinking*. Boston: Allyn and Bacon, 1991.
The author of this book has developed the spiral model of thinking in which basic cognitive processes such as determining relevance or discerning meaning are considered enabling skills. These enabling skills make possible the five developmental processes of classification, concept development, deriving principles, drawing conclusions and making generalizations. Of particular help to scholars in religious studies are the chapters on questions as a teaching tool and classroom discussions.

Shen, Fan A. "Teaching Critical Thinking In Freshman Composition." *Inquiry: Critical Thinking Across The Disciplines* 11 No. 4 (May, 1993): 14–16.
Shen sees critical thinking as a complex intellectual process involving several different thinking skills. To help students learn basic critical thinking skills, the author uses the debate format, which consists of three steps: (1) selection and initial exploration of a subject; (2) library research and reading and (3) debate, drafting and revision.

Sutherland, Tracey E., and Charles C. Bonwell, eds. *Using Active Learning in College Classes: A Range of Options for Faculty*. San Francisco: Jossey-Bass Publishers, 1996.

This book contains seven essays on various aspects of active learning. There is an excellent essay on using electronic tools (E-mail, the Internet) to promote active learning and one on writing as active learning. Other essays deal with the various barriers to active learning, the impact of classroom environments, the creation of inclusive classrooms, and the role of active learning in assessment.

Walters, Kerry S. "Critical Thinking in Liberal Education: A Case of Overkill?" *Liberal Education* 72 No. 3 (Fall, 1986): 233–244.
Speaks about the importance of writing to learn strategies such as keeping a journal, brainstorming and free writing.

Wilson, Brent G., ed. *Constructivist Learning Environments: Case Studies in Instructional Design*. Englewood Cliffs, NJ: Educational Technology, 1996.
According to Wilson, a "constructivist learning environment" is a place where meaningful activities help students construct understandings and develop skills relevant to solving problems. The three types of constructivist learning environments are: 1. computer microworlds; 2. classroom-based learning environments; and 3. open virtual learning environments. Two to three chapters describe specific examples of these three types. This book contains a plethora of ideas and examples concerning the constructivist learning environment. For scholars in religious studies I suggest reading Part Two before part One in order to ease the transition into the constructivist milieu.

Three Levels of Learning

Barnett, Ronald. *Improving Higher Education Total Quality Care*. Buckingham, England: SRHE and Open University Press, 1992.
Argues that critical thinking has more of a role to play in relation to the liberal disciplines than in regard to the operational ones. Barnett sees the teacher as a reflective practitioner.

Beyer, Barry K. "Hints for Improving the Teaching of Thinking in Our Schools: A Baker's Dozen." *Institute for Critical Thinking Resource Publication Series* No. 4. Montclair State College, Montclair, New Jersey, 1988: 1–7.
Makes the point that attention to thinking is for all students and that thinking is hard work.
———. *Practical Strategies For The Teaching Of Thinking*. Boston: Allyn And Bacon, Inc., 1987.
Beyer gives a rationale for the teaching of thinking and provides instruction directly in thinking. He endeavors to close the gap between what research suggest we do to teach thinking effectively and what generally occurs in classrooms now to accomplish this task.

Brookfield, Stephen D. *Becoming a Critically Reflective Teacher*. San Francisco: Jossey-Bass Publishers, 1995.

The author reflects on the meaning of being a critically reflective teacher. It means, in part, seeing ourselves through our students' eyes, unpacking the assumptions faculty make about their teaching and keeping a teaching log. Brookfield also discusses the cultural barriers to critical reflection such as the culture of silence, the culture of individualism and the culture of secrecy.

Bruer, John T "The Mind's Journey From Novice to Expert." *American Educator* 17 No. 2 (Summer, 1993): 6–15; 38–46.
The author defines learning as the process whereby novices become more expert in a particular discipline. Sees "chunking" or the extensive knowledge base of perceptual patterns as the key difference between novice and expert performance. Expertise depends on highly organized, domain-specific knowledge that arises only after extensive experience and practice in the domain.

Bruner, Jerome S. *The Process of Education.* Cambridge: Harvard University Press, 1961.
Argues that it is important to teach the structure of a discipline rather than an aggregate of unrelated facts.

Caissy, Gail A. "Curriculum For the Information Age." *Educational Horizons* 68 No. 1 (Fall, 1989): 42–45.
Teaching thinking skills must be both deliberate and continuous if students are to learn *how* to learn. Research in cognitive skill development demonstrates that if students are taught and given opportunities to practice basic thinking skills, their overall ability to solve problems (and to think) will improve.

Clarke, John H. and Arthur W. Biddle. *Teaching Critical Thinking: Reports from Across the Curriculum.* Englewood: Prentice Hall, 1993.
Contains 27 essays on various aspects of teaching critical thinking in various disciplines. Elizabeth Stroble's essay, "Belief and Doubt: Testing Concepts in Religious Studies," is pertinent to faculty who teach in the area of religious studies.

Cleveland, Harlan. "Educating for the Information Society." *Change* 17 No. 4 (July–August, 1985): 12–21.
Stresses the need for integrative thinking arguing that our educational system is geared more to categorizing and analyzing patches of knowledge rather than threading them together. The author predicts that those who stop learning will become peasants in the information society and that societies which fail to give all an education will be left in the jetstream of history by those that do.

Costa, Arthur, ed. *Developing Minds: A Resource Book for Teaching Thinking.* Alexandria: Association for Supervision and Curriculum Development, 1985.
Discusses such topics as creating school conditions for thinking programs for teaching thinking, assessing growth in thinking abilities, and

resources for teaching thinking. Particularly instructive are the appendices on A Thinking Skills Checklist, Suggestions for Getting Started, and A Glossary of Cognitive Terminology. Although not aimed at higher education this book can be adapted to serve the teaching of religious studies on the undergraduate level.

Cushing, K. S., et al. "Olympic Gold." *Educational Horizons* 70 No. 3 (Spring, 1992): 108–114.
As opposed to beginning teachers, expert and experienced teachers plan for, and deliver, instruction differently than do neophytes. Expert teachers focus on the interactive nature of learning and know what is normal student behavior. Thus they know, almost automatically, how to handle a wide range of classroom situations.

Floyd, Deborah Martin and Kathryn P. Scott. "Enhancing Critical Thinking Using The Case Study Method." *Inquiry: Critical Thinking Across the Disciplines* 8 No. 4 (Dec. 1991): 11–13.
Maintains that critical thinking abilities and dispositions are taught separately from the presentation of content in existing subject-matter offerings. Argues that critical thinking abilities and dispositions are generic and hence can be applied to a host of subject areas.

Garner, Ruth. *Metacognition and Reading Comprehension*. Norwood: Ablex Publishing Co., 1987.
The only way classrooms will become arenas for extensive strategy instruction is for the strategy instruction to be wholly intertwined with subject-area instruction as described in this book. Garner argues that the failure to teach strategies from which students could benefit is to risk that students will not become effective independent learners.

Garrison, Roger H. "The Tools of the Teaching Trade." *Improving College and University Teaching* 24 (1976): 69–72.
Argues that it is more important to teach students skills than it is to fill them with subject matter. The author asserts that the most important student question is: "Of what use is this course to me? What can I do with this knowledge?"

Glasser, William. "The Quality School Curriculums." *Phi Delta Kappan* 73 No. 9 (May, 1992): 690–694.
Maintains that tests should always show the acquisition of skills, never the acquisition of information alone. Understands skills as the ability to use knowledge and speaks of skills as "the outcomes that have value."

Grant, Grace E. *Teaching Critical Thinking*. New York: Praeger, 1988.
Argues that the process of teaching reasoning is a complex network of relations among a teacher's knowledge base, instructional decisions and classroom management and organization.

Grinola, Anne Bradstreet. *Critical Thinking: Reading Across the Curriculum*. Ithaca: Cornell University Press, 1984.

Memorizing a concept in isolation is not true mastery. One must be able to analyze, evaluate, apply, synthesize and translate the concept in one's own words. Grinola makes the point that students must read for ideas and answers rather than for word-for-word absorption.

Jones, Beau Fly, et al., eds. *Strategic Teaching and Learning: Cognitive Instruction in the Content Areas.* Alexandria: Association for Supervision and Curriculum Development, 1987.
Particularly helpful for professors of religious studies is Chapter Five, Strategic Teaching in Social Studies, which demonstrates how the insights gained from research on cognitive instruction can be applied to teaching social studies.

King, Patricia M., and Karen Strohm Kitchener. *Developing Reflective Judgement and Promoting Intellectual Growth and Critical Thinking in Adolescents and Adults.* San Francisco: Jossey-Bass Publishers, 1994.
Reflective thinking comes into play when there is awareness of a real problem or when there exists uncertainty about a solution. There are two main differences between critical thinking and reflective judgement: the epistemological assumptions on which the thinking person operates and the structure of the problem being addressed. This book describes the development of reflective thinking as found in the Reflective Judgement Model, provides evidence for the model and discusses its implications for college teaching and for student development.

Manning, Brenda H. and Beverly D. Payne. *Self-Talk for Teachers and Students: Metacognitive Strategies for Personal and Classroom Use.* Boston: Allyn and Bacon, 1995.
This book tries to link metacognition or "thinking about one's thinking" to the lives of teachers and students. It is the first book that demonstrates the importance of metacognition for teachers in one singular form. The authors give specific examples of how teachers can use metacognition for themselves in a powerful way, both personally and professionally. Although not intended for those who teach religious studies, the insights provided by this book may be applied to every discipline at any grade level.

Marzano, Robert J., et al., eds. *Dimensions of Thinking: A Framework for Curriculum and Instruction.* Alexandria: Association for Supervision and Curriculum Development, 1988.
Declarative, procedural and conditional knowledge are essential aspects of metacognition. Ideally, faculty should be able to identify these components for the task presented to students and to systematically teach and reinforce them.

Newman, Fred M. and Gary G. Wehlage. "Five Standards of Authentic Instruction." *Educational Leadership* 50 No. 7 (April, 1993): 8–12.
Makes the distinction between lower-order and higher-order thinking. The authors argue that when students engage in higher-order thinking, an element of uncertainty is introduced.

Perkins, David N., et al. *Smart Schools: From Training Memories To Educating Minds*. New York: The Free Press, 1992.
>   This book describes in broad strokes the contemporary science of teaching and learning that can inform teachers about how learning works best, focusing on factors that create positive energy in a school setting. Particular attention is given to the role of thoughtfulness in the teaching/learning process. This book may, *mutatis mutandis*, be fruitfully applied to the academic study of religion on the undergraduate level.

Powers, Donald E. and Mary K. Enright. "Analytical Reasoning Skills in Graduate Study." *The Journal of Higher Education* 58 No. 6 (Nov./Dec., 1987): 658–682.
>   Current educational practices do little to develop informal reasoning skills. Different skills are needed in different disciplines, e.g., the analysis and evaluation of arguments was judged to be most important in English while defining and analyzing problems was most important in computer science and engineering.

Smith, Robert M., et al. *Learning to Learn Across the Life Span*. San Francisco: Jossey-Bass Publishers, 1990.
>   The essay by Phillip C. Candy, "How People Learn to Learn," is particularly helpful.

Sternberg, Robert J. and Peter A. Frensch, eds. *Complex Problem Solving: Principles and Mechanisms*. Hillsdale: Lawrence Erlbaum Associates, Publishers, 1991.
>   Looks at problem solving and the differences between problem solving in experts and novices across a wide range of disciplines.

Strange, Carney. "Beyond the Classroom: Encouraging Reflective Thinking." *Liberal Education* 78 No. 1 (Jan./Feb., 1992): 28–31.
>   Argues that students need exposure to modes of reflective thinking more complex than ones currently held.

Thompson, Loren J. *Habits Of The Mind: Critical Thinking in the Classroom*. Lanham: University Press of America, Inc. 1995.
>   To ask whether education should stress subject matter or process skills amounts to casting up false and desperate alternatives. Education needs to emphasize the simultaneous learning of information and reasoning skills or process. In an age of information overload, the need to think with precision has become more critical than ever.

Weinert, Franz E. and Rainer H. Kluwe. *Metacognition, Motivation, and Understanding*. Hillsdale: Lawrence Erlbaum Associates, 1987.
>   This book will appeal to those who want an in-depth, sophisticated study of metacognition. It is more theoretical rather than practical in nature.

Woditsch, Gary A. with John Schmittroth. *The Thoughtful Teacher's Guide To Thinking Skills*. Hillsdale: Lawrence Erlbaum Associates, Publishers, 1991.

This entire book is aimed at classroom impact and has relevance for every grade level from K through graduate school. It demonstrates how instruction can be shared to improve thinking skills. The author argues that thinking skills instructors should set their sights on improving the skills of selective attention, sustained analysis, analoging, suspension of closure and autocensorship, skills that support the basic abilities of the mind to remember, discern and predicate.

Unsolved Mysteries

Baron, Joan Boykoff and Robert J. Sternberg, eds. *Teaching Thinking Skills: Theory and Practice*. New York: W.H. Freeman and Company, 1987.
An excellent collection of essays on various aspects of critical thinking. The essay by David Perkins on "Knowledge as Design," is particularly helpful. Perkins argues that teaching thinking through content dissolves the whole problem of transfer.

Brell, Carl D., Jr. "Critical Thinking as Transfer: The Reconstructive Integration of Otherwise Discrete Interpretations of Experience." *Educational Theory* 40 No. 1 (Winter, 1990): 53–68.

The foremost task in the teaching of critical thinking is less the transmission of any particular knowledge/skills than it is the fostering in students of those habits of reflective inquiry which lead to an ongoing disposition to seek intellectual, moral and social integrity, or what is referred to as "the critical spirit."

Downs-Lombardi, Judy. "Teaching Styles that Encourage (and Discourage) Thinking Skills. " *Inquiry: Critical Thinking Across the Disciplines* 15 No. 2 (Winter, 1995): 67–71.
When faculty promote thinking skills, they help students to see the rich subtleties and nuances of thought. Teaching styles that encourage thinking skills promote flexibility, relatedness, reciprocity and open-mindedness.

Heiman, Marcia and Joshua Slomianko, eds. *Thinking Skills Instruction: Concepts and Techniques*. Washington, D.C.: National Education Association, 1987.

Contains 35 essays on various aspects of critical thinking such as strategies for active involvement in problem solving, the transfer question and using literature to develop critical thinking skills.

Kahney, Hank. *Problem Solving: Current Issues*. 2nd ed. Buckingham, Philadelphia: Open University Press, 1993.
Most of what we know about learning and problem solving was discovered by analyzing the behavior of scholars solving "transformation problems," which are well-defined problems. However, many problems are only vaguely defined and the solver must help define the problem. Kahney argues that the way one represents a problem strongly influences the ease with which the problem can be solved.

Leithwood, Kenneth and Rosanne Steinbach. *Expert Problem Solving: Evidence from School and District Leaders*. Albany: State University of New York Press, 1995.
> This book pieces together much of what we have learned about expert administrative thinking and problem solving. Although it does not deal with teaching, per se, it sheds important light on the nature of problem solving for school administrators.

Penaskovic, Richard and Richard Ognibene. "Teaching: Some Affective Strategies." *Horizons: The Journal of the College Theology Society* 8 No. 1 (Spring, 1981): 97–108.
> Courses in theology can be structured in ways that eliminate the cognitive-affective dichotomy, while providing experiences whose motivational appeal enhances dialogue and the prospect of individual growth. Special attention is given to ways of structuring the classroom experience so that students become responsible for their own learning, activities designed to enhance the self-concept and methods for developing interpersonal communication skills that promote effective group discussion.

Perkins, David N., et al. *Thinking: The Second International Conference*. Hillsdale: Lawrence Erlbaum Associates, 1987.
> Contains thirty essays on various aspects of thinking such as contexts of thinking, theoretical perspectives on the teaching of thinking and designs for the teaching of thinking. There is an essay on the human brain as a model for decision making, post-logical thinking and "transfer" and teaching thinking.

Phelan, Patricia et al. "Speaking Up: Students' Perspectives on School." *Phi Delta Kappan Journal* 73 No. 9 (May, 1992): 695–704.
> Report of a study done at the Center for Research on the Context of Secondary School Teaching at Stanford University. Sheds light on the nature of environments that foster positive learning experiences. Points out that students want classes with their friends so that they feel less isolated and vulnerable.

Raths, Louis E., et al. *Teaching For Thinking: Theory, Strategies and Activities for the Classroom*. New York and London: Teachers College Press, Columbia University, 1986.
> Argues that most school exercises require a single correct answer, however, students are not able to answer a question that is outside the domain of their curriculum, and cannot extend their thinking into new territory. I especially recommend Part 4 "The Role of the Teacher" which treats teacher-student interactions, learning to watch ourselves teach and the implications of teaching for thinking.

Scheid, Karen. *Helping Students Become Strategic Learners: Guidelines for Teaching*. Cambridge: Brookline Books, 1993.
> Contains an excellent discussion of cognitive theories of learning and how they influence instructional decision making.

Sotillo, Susana. "Critical Thinking In The Content-Based Classroom: A Prelimi-
nary Study." *Inquiry: Critical Thinking Across The Disciplines* 8 No. 1
(September, 1991): 10–13.
Creating a non-threatening environment for student input would seem
to be a prerequisite for encouraging critical thinking.

Sternberg, Robert J. "Thinking Styles: Keys To Understanding Student Performance." *Inquiry: Critical Thinking Across The Disciplines* 7 No. 3 (April,
1991): 1; 32–35.
Learning styles are ways in which individuals prefer to use their intelligence or ways of directing the intellect that people find comfortable.
Identifying, developing and understanding thinking styles are tasks as
important as assessing, developing and understanding intelligence.

West, Charles K., James A. Farmer and Phillip M. Wolff, eds. *Instructional Design:
Implications From Cognitive Science.* Englewood Cliffs: Prentice Hall, 1991.
An excellent presentation concerning the implications of research on
cognitive strategies for instructional design.

Whiteman, Neal A. *Peer Teaching: To Teach is to Learn Twice.* Washington, D.C.:
George Washington University, 1988.
Asserts that learning is enhanced when it is more like a team effort,
rather than a solo race.

What is Critical Thinking?

Bloom, Alan. *The Closing of the American Mind.* New York: Simon and Schuster
Inc., 1987.
Where the Great Books are part of the curriculum, students feel they
are getting something from the university they cannot get elsewhere.
Students derive a fund of shared experiences and thoughts on which to
ground their friendships with one another.

Bok, Derek. *Higher Learning.* Cambridge: Harvard University Press, 1986.
Argues that knowledge alone does not suffice. The ability to think
clearly about complex problems is more important than knowledge
alone. A critical mind nourished by humane values may be the most
important product of education in a changing, fragmented society.
———. *Universities and the Future of America.* Durham and London: Duke University Press, 1990.
Argues that universities can contribute indirectly but significantly to
make our economy stronger and our society more humane.

Bowen, Howard R. *The State of the Nation and the Agenda for Higher Education.* San
Francisco: Jossey-Bass, 1982.
The body of requisite knowledge has become so vast that one can only
master a small segment of it. So in the popular mind, an educated
person is now a specialist. We no longer have a single conception of the
educated person but as many as there are specialties.

Brookfield, Stephen D. *Developing Critical Thinkers*. San Francisco: Jossey-Bass Publishers, 1987.
Critical thinking is a process not an outcome. It means to critically question assumptions; and it is not an entirely rational process because feelings and emotions enter into the process.

Chaffee, John. *Thinking Critically*. Boston: Houghton Mifflin Company, 1985.
A very helpful book, one based on classroom practice with lots of examples. Recommended for those new to the use of critical thinking in the classroom.

Capps, Walter H. *Religious Studies: The Making of a Discipline*. Minneapolis: Fortress Press, 1995.
This book illustrates what it means to think critically in religious studies. The author deals with such topics as the definition of religion, its origin or how it came into being, the description of religion, the purpose or function of religion, religious language, religious pluralism and the future of religion. Capps concludes that religious studies is a dynamic, ever-changing subject-field within which certain topics are looked at from many methodological sets of interest.

De Bono, Edward. *Masterthinker's Handbook*. New York: International Center for Creative Thinking, 1985.
Defines thinking as using one's mind to deal with a given situation. Distinguishes between active and reactive thinking. Makes a very helpful analogy between thinking and the parts of the human body. The "bones" are the key elements in an article or book. The "muscle" refers to the force or power of the thinking. The "fat" deals with the padding. Argues that effective thinking should be slim and trim.

Elliot, Norbert, et al. "Designing A Critical Thinking Model For A Comprehensive Technological University." *Inquiry: Critical Thinking Across the Disciplines* 7 No. 4 (May, 1991): 1–9.
The authors argue the thesis that an articulated critical thinking model has the potential to both unify and strengthen the curriculum. Critical thinking can enhance key areas of the curriculum with an engaging model tied to the mission of a particular university.

Facione, Peter A. "Toward a Theory of Critical Thinking." *Liberal Education* 70 No. 3 (Fall, 1984): 253–261.
To think critically means to be able to provide reasons for what one believes within that area of interest. Reasoning is a broader concept than critical thinking. All critical thinking is good reasoning, but not vice versa.

Farley, Edward. *The Fragility of Knowledge*. Philadelphia: Fortress Press, 1988.
Each of the five cultures of a university (the administrative complex, the medical, the athletic, the sciences and the humanities) has its own aims, ethos, language and power base. Makes some useful distinctions between a science, a discipline and specialty fields.

Follman, John. "Critical Thinking Definitions." *Inquiry: Critical Thinking Across The Disciplines* 8 No. 2 (October, 1991): 4–5.
   The author surveys definitions of critical thinking proposed by Sternberg, Ennis, Lipman and Perkins. Follman likes the definition of critical thinking provided by psychometricians which considers such components of critical thinking as deductive reasoning, evaluation of evidence, recognition of assumptions, evaluation of arguments and the reliability of statements.

Fuller, Timothy, ed. *The Voice of Liberal Learning. Michael Oakeshott on Education.* New Haven London: Yale University Press, 1989.
   Writes eloquently about the university as a home of learning, a place where a tradition of learning is both preserved and extended.

Girle, Roderic A. "Dialogue and the Teaching of Reasoning," *Educational Philosophy and Theory* 23 No. 1 (1991): 45–55.
   The author makes some comments about student needs and then proposes a broad based approach to the teaching of reasoning. The dialogical approach to teaching reasoning gives a broad framework into which a large number of ideas can be fitted. It also furnishes a framework for the assessment of student needs and for teaching critical reasoning skills.

Goodman, William M. "Critical Thinking For Adults: Can It Be Taught?" *Inquiry: Critical Thinking Across The Disciplines* 10 No. 2 (October, 1992): 9–11.
   The author wants to teach adult learners to think critically. Goodman understands "good judgement" to mean the ability to make wise decisions both conceptually and practically. Researchers are desperately needed today to teach the techniques of thinking remediation to adults.

Hanford, George. "Critical Thinking: A Field, A Discipline, A Subject, Or A Competency?" *Inquiry: Critical Thinking Across The Disciplines* 11 No. 4 (May, 1993): 13.
   The real impetus for the critical thinking movement came from its pertinence to the educational reform movement and not from its conception as a discipline or as a subject. Critical thinking is, first and foremost, a competency.

Hirsch, Eric Donald. *Cultural Literacy: What Every American Needs To Know.* Boston: Houghton-Mifflin Company, 1987.
   Cultural literacy refers to the network of information that competent readers possess. It is the background information stored in their minds, that enables them to read a newspaper with an adequate level of comprehension and relating what they read to the unstated context which alone gives meaning to what they read. To understand what someone says, we must understand more than the surface meaning, we have to understand the context as well. Hirsch argues that we have ignored cultural literacy in education because we have taken it for granted.

Hoaglund, John. "Landmarks in Critical Thinking Series: Ennis on the Concept of Critical Thinking." *Inquiry: Critical Thinking Across The Disciplines* 15 No. 2 (Winter, 1995): 1–19.
> Shows how Robert Ennis' concept of critical thinking (which appeared in the *Harvard Educational Review* in 1962) has changed over the years.

Kline, Stephen Jay. *Conceptual Foundations For Multi-Disciplinary Thinking.* Stanford: Stanford University Press, 1995.
> Argues that our intellectual system is severely fragmented and lacks a view of the whole. Offers a viewpoint we can use to understand the appropriate relationships among the various disciplines of knowledge. A highly sophisticated book in the new area of "multidisciplinary discourse."

Kowalski, Stephen. "Critical Thinking For Understanding." *Inquiry: Critical Thinking Across The Disciplines* 6 No. 2 (October, 1990): 8–9.
> The author reports on a workshop dealing with critical thinking. The trademarks of critical thinkers are generalization, the ability to discriminate relevant factors, model building, problem formulation and solution, and self-regulation.

Kurfiss, Joanne G. *Critical Thinking: Theory, Research, Practice, and Possibilities.* ASHE-ERIC Higher Education Report No.2. Washington, D.C.: Association for the Study of Higher Education, 1988.
> Summarizes cognitive research on thinking in various disciplines and describes courses that foster critical thinking in various disciplines.

Meehan, Eugene J. *The Thinking Game: A Guide to Effective Study.* Chatham: Chatham House Publishers, Inc. 1988.
> Defines thinking as the processes by which knowledge is developed, acquired, tested and applied. Makes a distinction between everyday knowledge and scientific knowledge based on the purposes for which knowledge is employed.

Neusner, Jacob. *How To Grade Your Professors.* Boston: Beacon Press, 1984.
> A thought-provoking book on teaching and learning by a scholar in religious studies. Maintains that true achievement depends on depth of learning, one's capacity for clear thinking, the ability to pursue knowledge where curiosity leads and the implacable criticism of all givens.

Paul, Richard. *Critical Thinking: What Every Person Needs to Survive in a Rapidly Changing World.* Rohnert Park: Sonoma State University, 1990.
> Contains some good ideas but this book could have used a good editor.

Postman, Neil. *The End of Education.* New York: Alfred A. Knopf, 1995.
> Students are bored and demoralized not because teachers lack interesting methods but because they and their teachers lack a "narrative" to provide a deeper meaning to their lessons. Narratives are a special genre of story-telling that uses history to give form to ideals. In Part I of this book, Postman speaks about five narratives which give a *raison*

d'etre for school. Part II provides levels of specificity to the narratives found in Part I. The author concludes that public schools exist to find and promote large, inclusive narratives for all students to believe in.

Rich, Morton D. "On Writing." *Inquiry: Critical Thinking Across The Disciplines* 10 No. 1 (September, 1992): 2.
Rich states that being open about how we think in our disciplines invites students into the process, thus reducing the mystery for them. He suggests that faculty write their own operational definition of critical thinking.

Sanford, Nevitt. *Where Colleges Fail: A Study of the Student as a Person.* San Francisco: Jossey-Bass, 1967.
Educational growth does not depend on the number of lectures attended. The faculty must reach the students. Dramatic changes can begin the moment there is a real encounter between teacher and student.

Scriven, Michael. "Critical for Survival." *National Forum: The Phi Kappa Phi Journal* 8 No. 1 (September, 1991): 10–13.
Argues that training in critical thinking should be the primary task of education.

Siegel, Harvey. "The Generalizability of Critical Thinking." *Educational Philosophy and Theory* 23 No. 1 (1991): 18–30.
Addresses the question concerning the generalizability of the skills and criteria which constitute an important part of the reason assessment component of critical thinking, and the question concerning the generalizability of the "critical spirit" component of critical thinking. The "critical spirit" for Ennis means a complex of attitudes, character traits, dispositions, and habits of mind.

Splitter, Laurance J. "Critical Thinking: What, Why, When and How." *Educational Philosophy and Theory* 23 No. 1 (1991): 89–109.
Argues that critical thinking needs to be incorporated into all levels of formal education. Urges that classrooms be transformed into communities of inquiry. Maintains that the development of thinking competence is as "basic" as the three R's.

Warren, Thomas, ed. *A View From The Academy: Liberal Arts Professors on Excellent Teaching.* Lanham: University Press of America, 1992.
This book includes twenty essays by liberal arts professors on various aspects of excellent teaching such as the teaching of quality, learning as conversation, teaching as a pilgrimage and teaching the humanities today.

Whitehead, Alfred North. *The Aims of Education and Other Essays.* New York: The Macmillan Company, 1929.
Maintains that universities preserve the nexus between knowledge and the zest of life, by uniting the young and the old in the imaginative

consideration of learning. Learning means watching the open pages of all the books we have ever read and, when the occasion arises, selecting the right page to read aloud to the universe.

Wicks, Robert J. "Clarity and Obscurity: Critical Thinking and Cognitive Therapeutic Principles in the Service of Spiritual Discernment." *Thought* 248 (March, 1988): 77–85.
Critical thinking derives from logic a method for generating questions about a given theme. From philosophy it derives a critically reflective, ethical and pragmatic attitude.

Wooley, William. "Preparation for Leadership: Student-Oriented Teaching in Liberal Arts Colleges." *A View From The Academy: Liberal Arts Professors on Excellent Teaching* ed. Thomas Warren. Lanham: University Press of America, 1992: 148–155.
This article examines the linkage between effective teaching and the liberal arts tradition. The purpose of liberal arts colleges is to train students to take leadership positions in a democratic society. The author's history courses are designed to be sets of experiences rather than packages of knowledge. What the author says about history courses may, *mutatis mutandis*, be applied to the academic study of religion.